Grade 5

Practice Book B

B

The McGraw-Hill Companies

Macmillan McGraw-Hill

Published by Macmillan/McGraw-Hill, of McGraw-Hill Education, a division of The McGraw-Hill Companies, Inc., Two Penn Plaza, New York, New York 10121.

Printed in the United States of America

4 5 6 7 8 9 10 005 09 08 07

Contents

Unit 1 • Challenges

Unit 2 • Discoveries

Unit 3 • Turning Points

Unit 4 • Experiences

Unit 5 • Achievements

Unit 6 • Great Ideas

Name ________________________________

soggy	categories	strands	capable
slumped	gigantic	luminous	credit

Suppose that you have just signed up to take part in a talent contest. Write a story about what happens before, during, and after the contest. Use as many of the words listed above as you can.

Name ______________________________

In "The Talent Contest," Danny is concerned, as he explains to his friend Elena, that he doesn't know what he's going to do for the talent contest. Suppose that instead of being unhappy, Danny is confident about his skills. How might Elena react if Danny were optimistic about the talent contest? Using these ideas, write a new story that includes Danny's and Elena's conversation. Then write about what might happen during the contest. Add character details.

___

___

___

___

___

___

___

___

___

___

___

___

___

___

___

___

___

___

___

___

At Home: Describe the difference in plot between your story and "The Talent Contest."

Name ______________________________

As you read *Miss Alaineus,* fill in the Character and Plot Chart.

Character	Plot

How does the information you wrote in this Character and Plot Chart help you analyze the story structure of *Miss Alaineus*?

At Home: Have the student use the chart to retell the story.

Name ______________________________

As I read, I will pay attention to pauses and breaks in the text.

The first thing readers should understand is this: I don't normally do
12 journals. My friend Lucy Matsuko, on the other hand, is capable of filling
25 up a book each month. It can be puffy and pink, or fitted with a heart-
41 shaped lock, or one of those old marbled notebooks you buy at the
54 drugstore. And everything goes on those pages—every boring thought or
65 mundane occurrence. No offense, Luce, if you're reading this.
74 But sometimes, an event comes along that changes everything. When
84 that happened to me, I had to write it all down. There had to be some kind
101 of official record.
104 Technically, I suppose, what you're about to read isn't just a journal.
116 It's really more like a scrapbook—which makes it more than just my
129 story. Anything that anyone had to say about it got thrown in here
142 (accompanied, of course, by my running commentary).
148 It all happened last spring, and I put this book together this summer,
161 while the whole thing was fresh in my mind. 170

Comprehension Check

1. How does the narrator feel about most journals? **Character**

2. Why did the narrator change his mind about writing a journal? **Plot and Character**

	Words Read	–	Number of Errors	=	Words Correct Score
First Read		–		=	
Second Read		–		=	

At Home: Help the student read the passage, paying attention to the goal at the top of the page.

Name ____________________

Photographs and **captions** give visual examples that help explain what the text states.

Look at the drawing and read the caption. Write a paragraph that explains what is happening.

Fifth graders learn about fitness and health by running a one mile race.

____

____

____

____

____

____

____

At Home: Look at several books, and describe how photographs and captions add to the stories.

Name ______________________________

Rewrite the sentences below, using a synonym from the word box for each underlined word.

weary	inevitable	handsome	courageous	heap
reside	furious	master	gigantic	category

1. The man on the cover of the magazine was good looking. ______________________________

2. The brave woman helped save the children. ______________________________

3. Put those words in that group. ______________________________

4. When she was left out, Jenna became angry. ______________________________

5. After the long climb, everyone was tired. ______________________________

6. A pile of coins sat on Grandpa's desk. ______________________________

7. Isabel could not wait to see what was inside the huge box. ______________________________

8. That's the house where I used to live. ______________________________

9. Students need to learn everything on this page. ______________________________

10. The dark clouds made a rainstorm seem certain. ______________________________

At Home: Work with a family member. Make a list of ten words that you hear at home, and write synonyms for them.

Name ______________________

The letters *a, e, i, o,* and *u* usually stand for the short vowel sounds /a/ in *damp*, /e/ in *ten*, /i/ in *sit*, /o/ in *hop*, and /u/ in *fun*. Some words with short vowel sounds do not follow this pattern. For example, *ea*, as in *head*, can have the /e/ sound and *ou* followed by *gh*, as in *rough*, can have the /u/ sound.

A. Underline the letter or letters that have the short vowel sound in each word. Then write another word that has the same short vowel sound in the same way.

1. lunch ______________

2. ship ______________

3. match ______________

4. odd ______________

5. spent ______________

6. tough ______________

7. knock ______________

8. myth ______________

9. graph ______________

10. bread ______________

B. Sort the words above into the different catagories.

short a

1. ______________

2. ______________

short e

3. ______________

4. ______________

short i

5. ______________

6. ______________

short o

7. ______________

8. ______________

C. Write a brief paragraph using some of the words from part A.

____

____

____

____

____

At Home: Name and write an additional word for each short vowel sound shown above. Underline the letter or letters that spell the sound.

Name ___________________________________

Read each clue below to complete the crossword puzzle. Choose from the words below.

advertisement	commenced	elected	fireball
impress	original	sauntered	wring

Across

1. Gain the respect of
4. Began
6. Public notice that is meant to persuade
7. Squeeze
8. Voted into office

Down

2. Walked slowly; strolled
3. A flaming sphere
5. First; earliest

Name ____________________

The **plot** of a story is the action that happens to the characters. The plot has a conflict, or a problem that the characters have to solve. The **setting** is where the story occurs.

Think about a fiction story you have read recently in which the setting is important. It might be a tall tale, a fairy tale, science fiction, or historical fiction. Answer the questions.

1. What is the title of the story? What was the story's setting? Why was the setting important to the plot? ____________________

2. Who is the main character in the story? What problem does the main character have to solve? ____________________

3. What were the important events in the plot? How did the main character solve the problem? ____________________

At Home: Find more examples of plot and setting in books or movies.

Name ________________________________

As you read *Davy Crockett Saves the World*, fill in the Plot and Setting Chart.

Plot	Setting

How does the information you wrote in this Plot and Setting Chart help you analyze the story structure of *Davy Crockett Saves the World*?

At Home: Have the student use the chart to retell the story.

Name ________________________________

As I read, I will pay attention to punctuation.

	Little Stormy sure loved the sea. Lots of folks figured
10	that he was born at sea—no one knew—but he certainly
22	made it his second home. Some days he'd dive into the water
34	and swim clear over to Boston and back, just for fun. Other
46	days, he'd hitch a ride on a passing whale. If he was lucky,
59	the whale would dive for the bottom, taking Stormy along
69	for the ride.
72	Stormy never meant to cause anyone trouble, but
80	accidents did happen. One day he dove into the sea but
91	didn't go headfirst. He tucked up his knees and did a sort
103	of cannonball. Well, wouldn't you know it, he caused giant
113	tidal waves in Rhode Island! Folks there got pretty flustered
123	until they discovered the cause. Then they just chuckled,
132	because even in Rhode Island they had heard about little
142	Stormy.
143	As Stormy grew older and bigger, he started to feel a
154	little cramped on Cape Cod. Stormy felt hemmed in by all
165	the cute little houses and villages. 171

Comprehension Check

1. What types of accidents did Stormy cause? **Plot**

2. Where do Stormy's adventures take place? **Setting**

	Words Read	–	Number of Errors	=	Words Correct Score
First Read		–		=	
Second Read		–		=	

At Home: Help the student read the passage, paying attention to the goal at the top of the page.

Name ______________________________

A **toolbar** is a strip of icons or symbols that allows you to visit different features on a Web site. A **link** is an electronic connection on a Web site that provides direct access to other documents or information.

Look at the tool bar and the two topics on the computer screen below. Answer the questions.

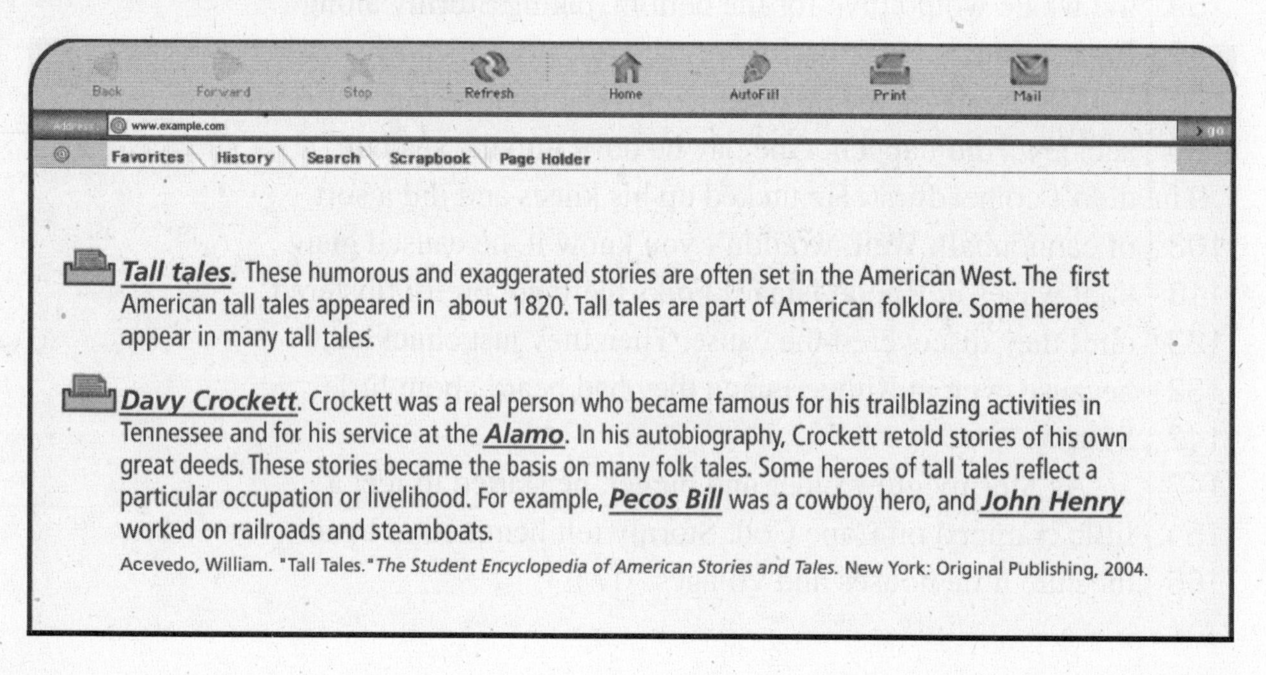

Tall tales. These humorous and exaggerated stories are often set in the American West. The first American tall tales appeared in about 1820. Tall tales are part of American folklore. Some heroes appear in many tall tales.

Davy Crockett. Crockett was a real person who became famous for his trailblazing activities in Tennessee and for his service at the ***Alamo***. In his autobiography, Crockett retold stories of his own great deeds. These stories became the basis on many folk tales. Some heroes of tall tales reflect a particular occupation or livelihood. For example, ***Pecos Bill*** was a cowboy hero, and ***John Henry*** worked on railroads and steamboats.

Acevedo, William. "Tall Tales." *The Student Encyclopedia of American Stories and Tales.* New York: Original Publishing, 2004.

1. What icon on the toolbar can you click to find more information about these topics or another topic? ______________________________

____

2. What link can you click on to find information about and examples of tall tales? How do you know it is a link? ______________________________

____

3. What links might you click on to find information about tall tale heroes other than Davy Crockett? ______________________________

____

At Home: Visit a trusted Web site with an adult to find more information about tall tales.

Name ____

A **compound word** is two or more words that appear together and have one meaning. A compound word can be written as one word, such as ***handbag,*** or as a hyphenated word, such as ***thirty-five.***

A. Draw a line to match each word in the first column with a word in the second column to form a compound word. Then write the new word. Use a dictionary to help you decide whether to write the word as one word or with a hyphen.

1. cheer	yard	____________
2. cannon	paper	____________
3. fifty	confident	____________
4. make	leader	____________
5. wheel	sauce	____________
6. every	believe	____________
7. self	body	____________
8. ship	seven	____________
9. news	chair	____________
10. apple	ball	____________

B. Write a paragraph using at least five compound words.

____

____

____

____

____

____

At Home: Name and write other compound words that contain the words *self, life, every,* and *ball.*

Name ________________________________

Words that have the VCe pattern usually have a long vowel sound, as in *fame*, *mine*, and *bone*. The vowel digraphs *ai* and *ay* can stand for the long *a* sound, as in *pail* and *play*. The digraphs *ee* and *ea* stand for the long *e* sound, as in *see* and *heap*. The digraphs *oa* and *ow* can stand for the long *o* sound, as in *boat* and *flow*. The vowel *i* can stand for the long *i* sound in words such as *wind*, *wild*. The letters *igh* in *high* can also stand for the long *i* sound.

A. Underline the letters that spell the long vowel sound in each word. Then write another word that spells the same long vowel sound in the same way.

1. greet ____________
2. made ____________
3. coach ____________
4. spice ____________
5. stray ____________
6. code ____________
7. bean ____________
8. narrow ____________
9. fighter ____________
10. aimless ____________
11. float ____________
12. grow ____________
13. toaster ____________
14. revoke ____________

B. Write a brief paragraph using the words from part A.

____

____

____

____

____

____

____

____

At Home: With a parent or helper, write another list of words that fit each spelling pattern.

Name ______________________________

A. Write the word from the box that belongs in each group.

major	settings	quest	buffet	reduce

1. goal, mission, ______________

2. lessen, minimize, ______________

3. important, great, ______________

4. places, areas, ______________

5. move, strike, ______________

B. Complete each sentence to show the meaning of the underlined word.

6. Pakenham went on a quest to ______________________________

______________________________.

7. Warm, sunny settings include ______________________________

______________________________.

8. Sometimes the waves buffet ______________________________

______________________________.

9. Park rangers try to reduce ______________________________

______________________________.

10. Major fires can ______________________________

______________________________.

Name ______________________________

- When authors compare two things, they tell how the things are alike.
- When authors contrast two things, they tell how the things are different.
- Signal words such as *both*, *alike, unlike, different, similarly,* and *on the other hand* help you identify when two things are being compared or contrasted.

Look at the information in the Venn Diagram. Then write a paragraph that has compare and contrast text structure.

Deciduous Trees	Alike	Coniferous Trees

____

____

____

____

____

At Home: Compare and contrast two animals by making a Venn Diagram and discussing their qualities with a parent or helper, using signal words.

Name ____

As you read "Forests of the World", fill in the Venn Diagram.

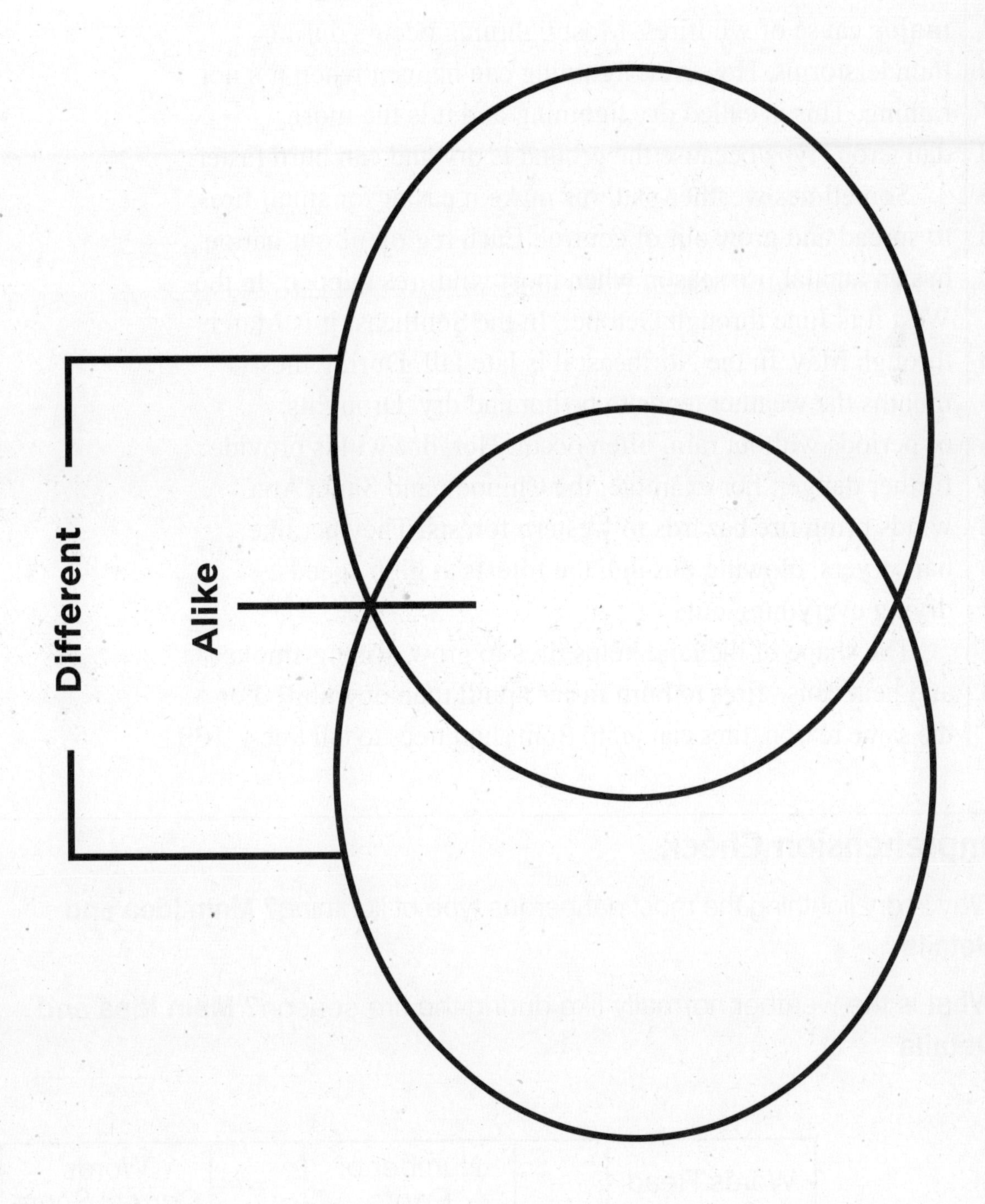

How does the information you wrote in this Venn Diagram help you analyze text structure of "Forests of the World"?

At Home: Have the student use the chart to retell the story.

Name ______________________________

As I read, I will pay attention to pronunciation.

Not all fires are started by people. Lightning is also a
11 **major** cause of wildfires. Most lightning occurs during
19 thunderstorms. However, lightning can happen when it's not
27 raining. This is called dry lightning and it is the most
38 dangerous type because the ground is dry and can burn faster.
49 Sometimes weather patterns make it easier for small fires
58 to spread and grow out of control. Each region of our nation
70 has an annual fire season when most wildfires happen. In the
81 West it is June through October. In the Southeast it is March
93 through May. In the Northeast it is late fall. During these
104 months the weather tends to be hot and dry. Droughts,
114 or periods without rain, often occur. Hot, dry winds provide
124 further danger. For example, the Chinook and Santa Ana
133 winds bring fire hazards to western forests. They act like
143 hair dryers, blowing through the forests at high speeds,
152 drying everything out.
155 The shape of the land helps fires to grow. Rising smoke
166 and heat cause fires to burn faster uphill than downhill. For
177 the same reason, fires can jump from short trees to tall trees. 189

Comprehension Check

1. Why is dry lightning the most dangerous type of lightning? **Main Idea and Details**

2. What is the weather normally like during the fire season? **Main Idea and Details**

	Words Read	–	Number of Errors	=	Words Correct Score
First Read		–		=	
Second Read		–		=	

At Home: Help the student read the passage, paying attention to the goal at the top of the page.

Name ______________________

To find an item in the **library** or **media center,** use the card catalog or online catalog. In both catalogs you can search by title, author, or subject. Online catalogs also allow you to search by key word.

When you go to the library, remember that items are arranged in a certain order. Works of fiction are arranged alphabetically by the author's last name. Works of nonfiction are arranged from lowest call number to highest call number. Periodicals (such as magazines) and nonprint materials (such as CDs) are kept in special areas.

Answer the questions about the library and media center.

1. You are looking for a book called *Blazing Bush and Forest Fires.* What are two ways to search a library catalog for this book? ______________________
____
2. In which section of the media center would you find a book about trees of North America? ______________
3. You are looking for a magazine that focuses on rain forests. In which section of the library would this magazine be kept? ______________
4. You know that Jean Craighead George has written a novel about a boy who lives in the woods, but you do not know the title. What are two ways that you could search for the novel? ______________________
____
____
____
5. You find a book that has a call number. In which section of the library should this book be shelved? ______________

At Home: List the names of five common items on a sheet of paper, and tell where you would find them in the media center.

Name ____

Homographs are two or more words that have the same spelling but different pronunciations or meanings.

Write the meaning of the boldfaced word in each sentence. Use a dictionary to help you.

1. There were four different kinds of salads at the **buffet.** ______________________________
2. The strong winds from the storm will **buffet** those small boats. ______________________________
3. Please sign and date the **contract.** ______________________________
4. Does water expand or **contract** when it is cold? ______________________________
5. The **object** in the museum case is from the first century. ______________________________
6. Because several people **object** to the new rule, we will change it. ______________________________
7. We hope to get a good grade on our social studies **project.** ______________________________
8. When you are on stage, you must **project** self-confidence. ______________________________
9. Please pick up some oranges and cucumbers in the **produce** section. ______________________________
10. If you are watching TV while doing homework, you will not **produce** good work. ______________________________

At Home: Have a parent or helper say each sentence with the boldfaced word omitted. Then say and spell the correct word.

Name ______________________________

The words below have the vowel sounds in l**oo**n, m**u**le, and b**oo**k.

truth	few	crook	smooth
fuel	stood	poodle	juice
produce	wood	strewn	menu
glue	foot	computer	acute
bamboo	brook	cruise	

A. Read the headings of the chart. Then write the words from the box in the correct column.

The /ü/ sound in loon		The /ū/ sound in mule	The /ů/ sound in book

B. Use your completed chart to write the different letter combinations that can be used to spell each sound.

1. the vowel sound in ***loon*** ______________________________

2. the vowel sound in ***mule*** ______________________________

3. the oo sound in ***book*** ______________________________

At Home: With a parent or helper, think of more words to add to your chart.

Name ______________________________

A. Complete each sentence with a word from the box.

mission	environment	gravity	maze
zone	adjusted	function	disasters

1. Scientists often have rats run through a ______________ to see if the rats can find food.
2. Astronauts must know the ______________ of each button in the space shuttle.
3. Space is a different ______________ from Earth, so astronauts need to adapt.
4. ______________ is a force that helps keep Earth in its orbit around the Sun.
5. Every member of a space mission is trained to avoid any ______________.
6. One day, there may be a ______________ to send astronauts to Mars.
7. The astronauts ______________ the heights of their chairs.
8. The launch ______________ must be safe and clear before a shuttle launches.

B. Think about a space mission that you have heard about. Write a paragraph describing the mission. Use as many of the vocabulary words as you can in your paragraph.

____

____

____

____

____

____

____

Name ______________________________

A summary is a short statement of the most important ideas in a selection. To summarize, find the main idea and the most important supporting details and restate them in your own words.

Choose a nonfiction article you have read or a section in your science textbook about the solar system. Write a summary including the main ideas and important details. Make sure you restate your summary in your own words.

____

____

____

____

____

____

____

____

____

____

____

____

____

____

____

____

____

____

At Home: Find an interesting newspaper or magazine article and summarize it. Share your summary with a parent or helper.

Name ______________________________

As you read *Ultimate Field Trip 5,* fill in the Summary Chart.

Main Ideas	Main Ideas	Main Ideas

Summary

How does the information you wrote in this Summary Chart help you generate questions about *Ultimate Field Trip 5*?

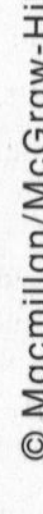

At Home: Have the student use the chart to retell the story.

Name ______________________________

As I read, I will pay attention to pronunciation.

When a space shuttle crew's job at the ISS is done, it undocks, fires
14 its thrusters, and heads back to Earth. Three crewmembers are left on
26 the ISS to work for the next four to six months.
37 One of the most important things the astronauts do is run
48 experiments. The ISS is running long-term studies on how human
58 bodies behave in a low **gravity environment**. This might involve
68 researching how people sleep. It might mean taking frequent blood
78 samples. These samples can show how a crewmember's body
87 chemistry is changing or how his or her immune system is responding
99 to living in a very enclosed space. The experiments also might involve
111 measuring a crewmember's bone density.
116 Another set of important experiments on the ISS studies how
126 various materials act in space. The results of these studies will help us
139 make better metals and materials to use in space.
148 While some astronauts are gathering data, others are working on
158 computers to record the results of their studies. 166

Comprehension Check

1. What are some experiments the astronauts run on the ISS? **Summarize**

2. How do the astronauts know if the experiments are successful or not? **Main Idea and Details**

	Words Read	–	Number of Errors	=	Words Correct Score
First Read		–		=	
Second Read		–		=	

At Home: Help the student read the passage, paying attention to the goal at the top of the page.

Name ______________________________

Rhyme schemes are the patterns of rhyming words in poems.
Rhythm is the regular repetition of accented syllables.

A. Write a line that rhymes with each line below.

1. I would like to fly

____

2. I'd like to visit space one day

____

3. A place with zero gravity

____

4. We will visit Mars

____

5. Outer space will prove a zone

____

B. Read the following lines from a poem. Then underline the accented syllables to find the rhythm.

The sun was shining on the sea,
Shining with all his might:
He did his very best to make
The billows smooth and bright.

At Home: Write a poem about space with a regular rhyme scheme and rhythm. You may also choose to continue the poem at the bottom of this page.

Name ______________________________

Read the paragraph. Then use context clues to write a definition for each underlined word.

The first few hours in space can cause a great deal of suffering and extreme discomfort for astronauts. Many of the problems result from the absence of gravity. Gravity is the force that holds us down on Earth, a bit like the way a tether holds a dog to a tree or post. Without gravity many unusual things happen. Blood rushes upward which causes astronauts' faces to become puffy and flushed. Veins in the face and neck can start pulsating hard enough for others to see the blood pumping. Astronauts may experience nausea, too, a sick feeling in the stomach. People also become disoriented in space. This confusion occurs because the brain's sense of balance is lost. Some effects of zero gravity are even more surprising. Gravity tends to compress and tighten us as it pulls us downward. Without gravity, people get a little taller. In fact, their bodies are altered slightly as their waists and legs thin out. With all of these changes, it is no wonder that people feel distressed and anxious during the first few hours without gravity.

1. **discomfort** ______________________________
2. **gravity** ______________________________
3. **tether** ______________________________
4. **flushed** ______________________________
5. **pulsating** ______________________________
6. **nausea** ______________________________
7. **compress** ______________________________
8. **disoriented** ______________________________
9. **altered** ______________________________
10. **distressed** ______________________________

At Home: Choose five of the words above, and write a new sentence for each of the words.

Name ____________________

A. Read the headings on the chart. Say the words in the box, and listen to their vowel and *r* sounds. Then write the words in the correct column of the chart.

explore	chart	starch	stares
gorge	uproar	marsh	harm
wearing	sparkplug	coarse	beware
scarce	swear	course	there

/är/ in *large*	/âr/ in *square*	/ôr/ in *core*

B. Use your completed chart to write the different letter combinations that can stand for each sound.

1. words with /är/ such as *large* ____________________
2. words with /âr/ such as *square* ____________________
3. words with /ôr/ such as *core* ____________________
4. Which word with the /âr/ sound does not follow the pattern? ____________

At Home: Make a chart showing some of the different ways to spell /är/ as in *large*, /âr/ as in *square*, and /ôr/ as in *core*.

Name ______________________________

Use your knowledge of the vocabulary words in bold type to answer each question. Answer in a complete sentence, and use the vocabulary word in your answer.

1. What is your favorite **celebration**? ______________________________

2. During your day at school, what might a **variety** of activities include?

3. What is one **fragrance** that you like? ______________________________

4. If a sponge is **moistened**, how does it feel when you touch it? __________

5. Why is **cooperation** important when solving problems in a group? ________

6. Why might an outdoor event be **canceled**? ______________________________

7. What is one way that water is **transformed**? ______________________________

8. What is a **theory** that people in the past had about the world? __________

Name ____

As you read, you often learn the reasons for events in a story. The reason that something happens is the **cause.** What happens as a result of a cause is the **effect.** Sometimes word clues help you see cause-and-effect relationships. Look for words such as ***because, so, therefore, since,*** and ***when*** that explain why an event happened.

Read the sentences below. Then write the cause and the effect on the lines provided. Underline any clue words in the sentences.

1. Because Lupe's house is on a mountainside, she has to walk downhill to school every day.

   Cause: ____

   Effect: ____

2. Pipiolo was eager to start the day, so he woke Lupe before the rooster crowed.

   Cause: ____

   Effect: ____

3. Pipiolo went out every night; therefore, he was tired during the day.

   Cause: ____

   Effect: ____

4. The roof dogs were happy when they saw Pipiolo.

   Cause: ____

   Effect: ____

5. Since she trusted Pipiolo, Chulita jumped onto the wagon.

   Cause: ____

   Effect: ____

At Home: Read a short story and identify the cause-and-effect relationships.

Name ______________________________

As you read *Pipiolo and the Roof Dogs,* fill in the Cause and Effect Chart.

Cause	→	Effect
	→	
	→	
	→	
	→	

How does the information you wrote in this Cause and Effect Chart help you generate questions about *Pipiolo and the Roof Dogs*?

At Home: Have the student use the chart to retell the story.

Name ______________________________

As I read, I will pay attention to tempo.

	"Wow!" Arlene said happily, as she stood back to admire
10	the jungle scene she and Aunt Violet had painted on a piece
22	of canvas. Arlene had to admit that they had done fantastic
33	work. "It's unbelievable! I'll get the stepladder so we can
43	hang it up!"
46	"My goodness, Arlene. Let the paint dry first!" Aunt
55	Violet said. "On a rainy day like this, that paint could take
67	a while to dry. While we're waiting, let's go over the list of
80	party foods. Now where did I put my glasses? I can't seem
92	to keep track of them!"
97	Arlene and Aunt Violet were finishing up the preparations
106	for a party that night. It was a birthday celebration for Arlene's
118	little brother, Gary. He loved wild animals, so Arlene and
128	Aunt Violet had transformed Aunt Violet's living room into
137	a jungle. There was even a cardboard giraffe peeking out
147	from behind the big red chair!
153	While Aunt Violet went over her list, Arlene glanced over
163	the room. It was turning out just as she had planned. 174

Comprehension Check

1. What are Arlene and Aunt Violet preparing for? **Plot**

2. What does the word ***transformed*** mean? **Context Clues**

	Words Read	–	Number of Errors	=	Words Correct Score
First Read		–		=	
Second Read		–		=	

At Home: Help the student read the passage, paying attention to the goal at the top of the page.

Name ______________________________

Charts arrange information in groups or categories. Always read the title of a chart first. Next read the headings of each column, or group arranged from top to bottom. Then read the information in each row. Rows are arranged from left to right.

Dog Adaptations		
Breed	**Adaptations**	**Job**
husky	thick fur, strong, fast	pulling sleds
collie	good eyesight, instinct for herding other animals	tending sheep and cattle
bloodhound	excellent sense of smell	searching and rescuing
greyhound	long, slim body and legs; fast and energetic	racing

Use the information in the chart above to write a paragraph explaining how each breed's job fits its adaptations. Be sure to begin your paragraph with a sentence that states the main idea.

____

____

____

____

____

____

____

____

____

____

At Home: Find a chart in a newspaper. Identify the title and explain to your parent or helper what information is shown in the columns and rows.

Name ___________________________

A thesaurus lists words and their **synonyms**. A dictionary lists words and their definitions, as well as synonyms.

A. Use a thesaurus or dictionary to find two synonyms for each word below. Make sure that the words and their synonyms are the same part of speech.

1. fragrance *n.* ___________________________

2. aroma *n.* ___________________________

3. waft *v.* ___________________________

4. pungent *adj.* ___________________________

5. odoriferous *adj.* ___________________________

6. reek *v.* ___________________________

7. perfume n. ___________________________

B. Write a sentence for pairs of synonyms in part A.

8. ___________________________

9. ___________________________

10. ___________________________

11. ___________________________

12. ___________________________

13. ___________________________

14. ___________________________

____

At Home: Ask a parent or helper to select five challenging words from a book or magazine. Use a thesaurus or dictionary to find a synonym for each of these words.

Name ______________________________

A. Say the words below, and listen to their vowel and *r* sounds. Write the words from the box in the correct column of the chart. Then add two more words to each column.

fear	dirty	beard	blurt
thirsty	rehearse	submerge	appear
unclear	pioneer	herd	engineer

/ûr/ in *fur*	**/îr/ in *gear***

B. Use your completed chart to write ways to spell each sound.

1. words with **/ûr/** such as *fur* ______________________________

2. words with **/îr/** such as *fear* ______________________________

At Home: Add three more words to each column of the chart above. Ask a parent or helper to check your work.

Name ______________________________

soggy	credit	advertisement	transformed	maze
reduce	luminous	sauntered	commenced	quest

A. Read each clue. Then write the matching vocabulary word on the line next to it.

1. glowing, or reflecting light ________________
2. Praise, something owed to a person ________________
3. began ________________
4. strutted ________________
5. a complicated series of passageways or paths ________________
6. a long, meaningful journey ________________
7. changed in form ________________
8. to make smaller ________________

function	mission	disasters	cooperation
variety	celebration	major	gigantic

B. Write a paragraph that includes six words from the box above.

____

____

____

____

____

____

____

Name ____________________

A. Write the correct vocabulary word from the box next to its meaning in each sentence.

soggy	canceled	mission	reduce	commenced	strands

1. Damp or wet ____________________
2. To decrease ____________________
3. Began or started ____________________
4. Assignment or quest ____________________
5. Ended, no longer occuring ____________________
6. Things similar to threads ____________________

advertisement	major	fragrance
original	capable	environment

B. Choose the word from the box that best completes each sentence below.

7. Although the ____________________ document was lost, we still had a good copy.
8. The ____________________ at summer camp is fun and friendly.
9. If we all work together, we are ____________________ of saving Earth's resources.
10. It will require a ____________________ effort to stop pollution, but people will succeed if everyone cooperates.
11. When flowers bloom, they give off a lovely ____________________.
12. During the television show, we saw an ____________________ for shampoo.

Name ______________________________

A. Circle the vocabulary word that correctly completes the sentence.

1. The staff's treatment of the hawk showed that they had (decency/shrieks).
2. The hawk's (sympathy/injury) was not too severe.
3. After (practicing/delivering) the hawk to the veterinarian, the child waited in the lobby.
4. The bird's(shrieks/decency) were very loud.
5. Children often become (sympathy/mournful) when they see injured animals.
6. A (bulletin board/injury) is a great place to put a picture.
7. She listened to her son (slurp/delivering) his smoothie.
8. A helpless, injured animal will fill anyone with (bulletin board/sympathy).

B. Read each sentence. If the vocabulary word is used correctly, write C on the line.

9. I took my dog to the vet because he had an **injury**. ___
10. People who have **decency** will care for an animal. ___
11. Anita was **mournful** when she helped the bird. ___
12. Ralph would often **slurp** his soda quietly. ___

Name ______________________________

You know that when you **make inferences**, you are filling in information that is not specifically stated in the text. You can fill in the missing information by finding clues from the text and by using your life experience or previous readings.

Read the excerpt from *Shiloh.* Then answer the questions.

Dad don't say much. He come home to find Shiloh there, he just stands off to one side, listening to what Doc Murphy said about him; he don't get close enough for Shiloh to take a lick. But when supper's over and I go off to the bathroom to brush my teeth, I peek back through the doorway, and Dad's over by Shiloh's box, letting him lick his plate clean. Dad crouches there a minute or two, scratching all down Shiloh's back and up again.

Inference from Text

1. Who is Shiloh? How do you know?

____

____

2. What job does Doc Murphy have? How do you know?

____

Inference from Life Experience/Previous Reading

1. Is Shiloh in good health? How do you know from your own life experience?

____

____

____

2. From your own life experience or from previous reading what inference can you make about someone who cannot bring his or her sick pet to the vet?

____

____

At Home: Think of an inference you have made at home. Write a brief paragraph about the inference.

Name ___________________________________

As you read *Shiloh,* fill in the Inferences Chart.

Text Clues	What You Know	Inferences

How does the information you wrote in this Inferences Chart help you monitor comprehension of *Shiloh*?

At Home: Have the student use the chart to retell the story.

Name ______________________________

As I read, I will pay attention to punctuation.

	From behind a curtain of trees came a low growl and then
12	a loud, angry bark. "What is it, Brett?" Chandra turned to
23	look. Fifty feet from their dog was a black bear. He looked
35	like a young bear, just a cub maybe.
43	Chandra tried to remember if you were supposed to
52	look a bear in the eye and scream or drop down and play
65	dead. And what were you supposed to do with your dog?
76	"Brett!" she shouted. But he just kept barking until the bear
87	backed off deeper into the woods. Chandra and Animesh
96	stared after the retreating bear.
101	"I think he's a stray," said Animesh.
108	"What makes you say that?" Chandra asked.
115	"Why else would he come to the edge of the woods?"
126	"Maybe he's hungry she said. Chandra knew you didn't
135	call a bear a stray, but she couldn't think of what else it
148	might be called. 151

Comprehension Check

1. How would you summarize the second paragraph of the passage? **Summarize**

2. Why does Chandra tell her dog to be quiet? **Make Inferences**

	Words Read	–	Number of Errors	=	Words Correct Score
First Read		–		=	
Second Read		–		=	

At Home: Help the student read the passage, paying attention to the goal at the top of the page.

Name ________________________________

A **photograph** can help you visually see what a story or article is explaining or describing. The photograph's **caption** provides more information about what you see in the photograph.

Study the photograph and read the caption and the article. Then beside each true statement, show where the information can be found by writing a C for caption, P for photo, or A for article on the line. Put an X next to statements which cannot be proved true.

The Third Street Animal Shelter, located on the corners of Third Street and Broadway, is holding an adoption fair from 9 a.m. to 7 p.m. today. Linda Bailey, the director of the shelter, invites families to stop by and visit the animals. "The fair will be like one big petting zoo with ten dogs, twelve puppies, five cats, and seven kittens waiting for adoption," she said. "And all pets adopted at the fair will be given free shots."

Richard Vitarelli, 11, chooses a beagle at the Third Street Adoption Fair.

1. _______ Ten dogs, five cats, seven kittens, and twelve puppies were up for adoption.
2. _______ The Third Street Animal Shelter is open from 9 a.m. to 7 p.m. daily.
3. _______ There was a clown giving out balloons and a cowboy offering free pony rides.
4. _______ The name of the boy petting the beagle is Richard Vitarelli.
5. _______ Eleven-year-old Richard adopted the beagle.
6. _______ At the fair, each animal was in its own crate.
7. _______ Free shots were given to the pets that were adopted.
8. _______ All the animals were adopted, except for a cat and two dogs.

At Home: Go through newspapers or magazines to find photographs and captions. Explain how the photographs help you understand more about the story.

Name ______________________________

A. Use a dictionary to help find the meanings of the idioms below. Then use each in a sentence.

1. Can't make heads or tails of it.

____

____

____

2. To hit it off.

____

____

____

3. To get up on the wrong side of the bed.

____

____

____

B. Write a paragraph using two of the idoms from the box.

To bite off more than one can chew
To catch on
To put the cart before the horse
To be on a wild-goose chase

____

____

____

____

____

At Home: Work together to find idioms in newspapers, books, or magazines.

Name ____________________

A. Write a story about taking care of an animal. Use the following compound words in your story.

playground	sidewalk	backyard
newspaper	homemade	haircut
breakfast	toothbrush	thunderstorm

____
____
____
____
____
____
____
____

B. Now make a list of other compound words you know. Use your list to write a silly story about animals.

____
____
____
____
____
____
____
____

At Home: Illustrate your story and share it with a parent or helper.

Name ______________________________

Write a sentence, using each of the vocabulary words below. Make sure that your sentence shows that you understand the meaning of the vocabulary word.

1. **vibrates** ______________________________

2. **surroundings** ______________________________

3. **species** ______________________________

4. **prey** ______________________________

5. **alert** ______________________________

6. **predators** ______________________________

7. **lunging** ______________________________

8. **survive** ______________________________

Name ______________________________

The **main idea** is the most important point the author is making in a passage. **Details** are facts that are added to support the main idea.

Read the paragraphs below. Underline the main idea in each and write the supporting details of the main idea on the lines below the passage.

The territory of the western diamondback rattlesnake extends from southern California across the tip of Nevada, through the southern half of Arizona to Texas, Oklahoma and Arkansas, and south to the interior of Mexico. They can be found in a wide range of habitats from coastal sand dunes to forests, to deserts, and even at altitudes of over 7,000 feet. They stand their ground when threatened, often strike repeatedly, and account for more serious and fatal snake bites than any other American snake. For these reasons, the western diamondback rattlesnake is considered the most dangerous reptile in North America.

1. ______________________________

____

Copperhead snakes should be considered a dangerous pest for rural families. Although its bite is rarely fatal, it is very painful. They can be expected to be seen in gardens, flower beds, and around houses. Copperheads prefer to eat small rodents and frogs which are attracted to the dampness that can be found around these areas.

2. ______________________________

____

The sidewinder, a small desert rattlesnake, is also called the "Horned Rattlesnake." It is light in color, ranging from tan, cream, pink, gray, or sandy-colored, with darker patches on its back. Its supraoculars, triangular projections over each eye, are pointed and upturned, giving them a horn-like appearance.

3. ______________________________

____

At Home: Read a magazine article and identify its main idea. Write an outline of the article.

Name ___________________________

As you read a section of "Rattlers!", fill in the Main Idea Web.

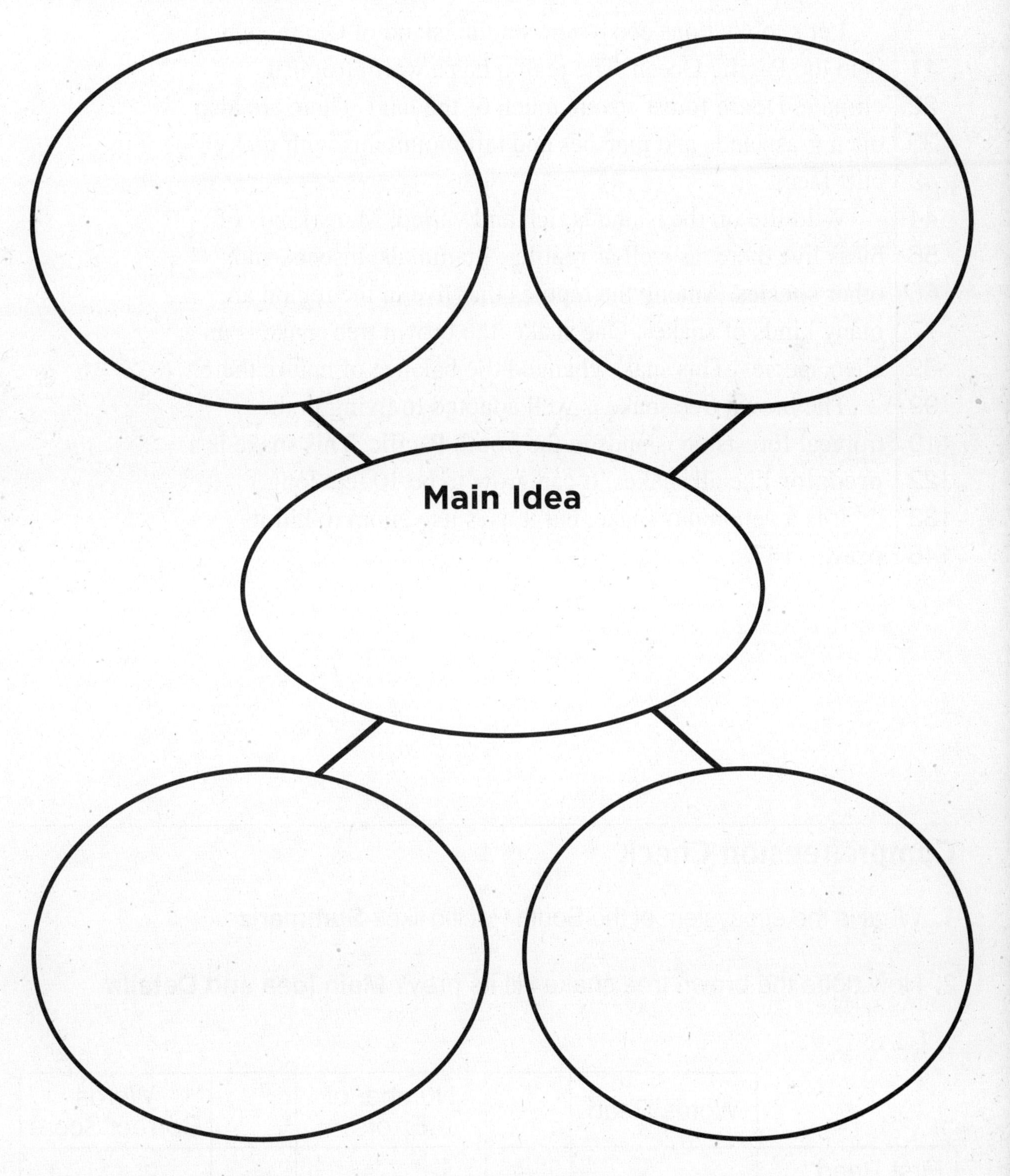

How does the information you wrote in this Main Idea Web help you summarize the section of "Rattlers!" you chose?

At Home: Have the student use the chart to retell the story.

Name ____________________

As I read, I will pay attention to punctuation.

Let's look at one ecosystem on the island of Guam, which
11 is in the Pacific Ocean. The region has a warm tropical
22 climate. Dense forest covers much of the land. There are also
33 open grasslands and marshes and tall mountains with rocky
42 cliff faces.
44 Wild life on the island is rich and varied. Many kinds of
56 birds live there, as well as reptiles, mammals, insects, and
66 other **species**. Among the reptiles that live in the region are
77 many kinds of snakes. One snake, the brown tree snake is an
89 alien species. This snake changed the balance of nature there.
99 The brown tree snake is well adapted to living in the
110 tropical forests on islands in the South Pacific. This snake is a
122 **predator** like all snakes. It can grow to be 10 feet long.
133 It is a venomous snake, but it uses its venom to kill its
146 **prey.** 147

Comprehension Check

1. What is the ecosystem of the South Pacific like? **Summarize**

2. How does the brown tree snake kill its prey? **Main Idea and Details**

	Words Read	–	Number of Errors	=	Words Correct Score
First Read		–		=	
Second Read		–		=	

At Home: Help the student read the passage, paying attention to the goal at the top of the page.

Name ____

Legends are stories that come down from the past, based on the traditions of a people or region. The **hero** is the main character in a legend, who often does something brave to help others. **Personification** is the assignment of human characteristics to an animal, a thing, or an idea.

Write a short legend that explains how the sky became blue. Make sure that your legend has a hero and includes the personification of at least one animal or thing.

____

____

____

____

____

____

____

____

____

____

____

____

____

____

____

____

____

____

At Home: Tell your legend to a family member or helper. Explain how you have personified an animal or thing and identify the hero.

Name ____________________

If you don't know a word, you can use the words surrounding it to help you define it. Defining a word this way is known as using **context clues.**

A. Read the sentences and then complete the chart.

1. Different kinds of rattlers live in different habitats, or environments. For example, sidewinders live in deserts, and many timber snakes live in rocky woodlands.

2. All the old skin is exuded, or comes off, when rattlesnakes shed.

3. After a snake injects its venom, or poison, its prey has little chance for survival.

4. Some predators, animals which capture rattlesnakes for food, include hawks, owls, and eagles.

Word	Context Clue	Definition
1. habitats		
2. exuded		
3. venom		
4. predators		

B. Write two sentences about snakes using context clues set off by a comma.

1. ____________________

____

2. ____________________

____

At Home: Read a story or an article, select five challenging words and define the words, using only context clues

Name ______________________________

To make most words plural, add **-s** to the singular form of the word. However, add **-es** to singular words that end in ***ch, sh, s, x,*** or ***z.*** When a singular word ends in a consonant and ***y,*** change the ***y*** to ***i*** and add ***-es.***

Write a sentence that contains the plural form of each word below. Underline all of the plural nouns in each sentence.

1. compass ______________________________

2. grassland ______________________________

3. eyelash ______________________________

4. enemy ______________________________

5. supply ______________________________

6. loss ______________________________

7. index ______________________________

8. highway ______________________________

9. ditch ______________________________

10. ability ______________________________

At Home: Write a newspaper article about an event at your school. Use at least six plural words.

Name ______________________________

Write a clue for each word in the crossword puzzle below. Make each clue a sentence with a blank where the word in the puzzle could go.

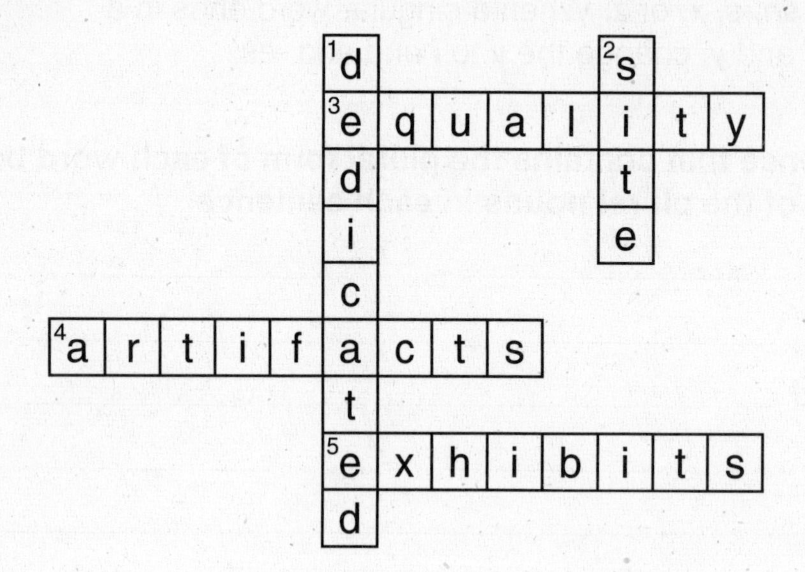

Across

3. ______________________________

4. ______________________________

5. ______________________________

Down

1. ______________________________

2. ______________________________

Name ______________________________

The **main idea** of an article or a story is the story's most important idea. **Details** support the main idea. When you summarize an article, you tell the main idea and supporting details.

Read the article below. In each paragraph, circle the main idea, underline the supporting details, and cross out any unnecessary information.

Maya Lin is one of a unique few who has managed to make a connection between art and architecture. Influenced by Earth artists of the 60s and 70s, she uses the notion of landscape in her work. "I work with the landscape, and I hope that the object and the land are equal partners," she says. Lin attended Yale University, and received a Bachelor of Arts degree in Architecture in 1981, and a Master of Architecture from Yale's School of Architecture in 1986. Since 1987 when she opened her studio, Lin has completed art and architecture projects designed for various locations in the United States.

Maya Lin has been the recipient of many awards. She has won the architecture prize from the American Academy of Arts and Letters for designing buildings like the Langston Hughes Library and the Museum for African Art in SoHo, New York. She has also received the Presidential Design Award, The American Institute of Architects Honor Award, and the Henry Bacon Memorial Award. Lin has won honorary doctorates in Fine Arts from Harvard, Yale, Brown, Smith, and Williams. She is currently working on sculpture installations for the Rockefeller Foundation Headquarters and the Cleveland Public Library.

At Home: Read an article about a well-known artist or social leader, and identify its main idea. Write a brief paragraph that summarizes the article.

Name ______________________________

As you read "Maya Lin: Architect of Memory," fill in the Main Idea Web.

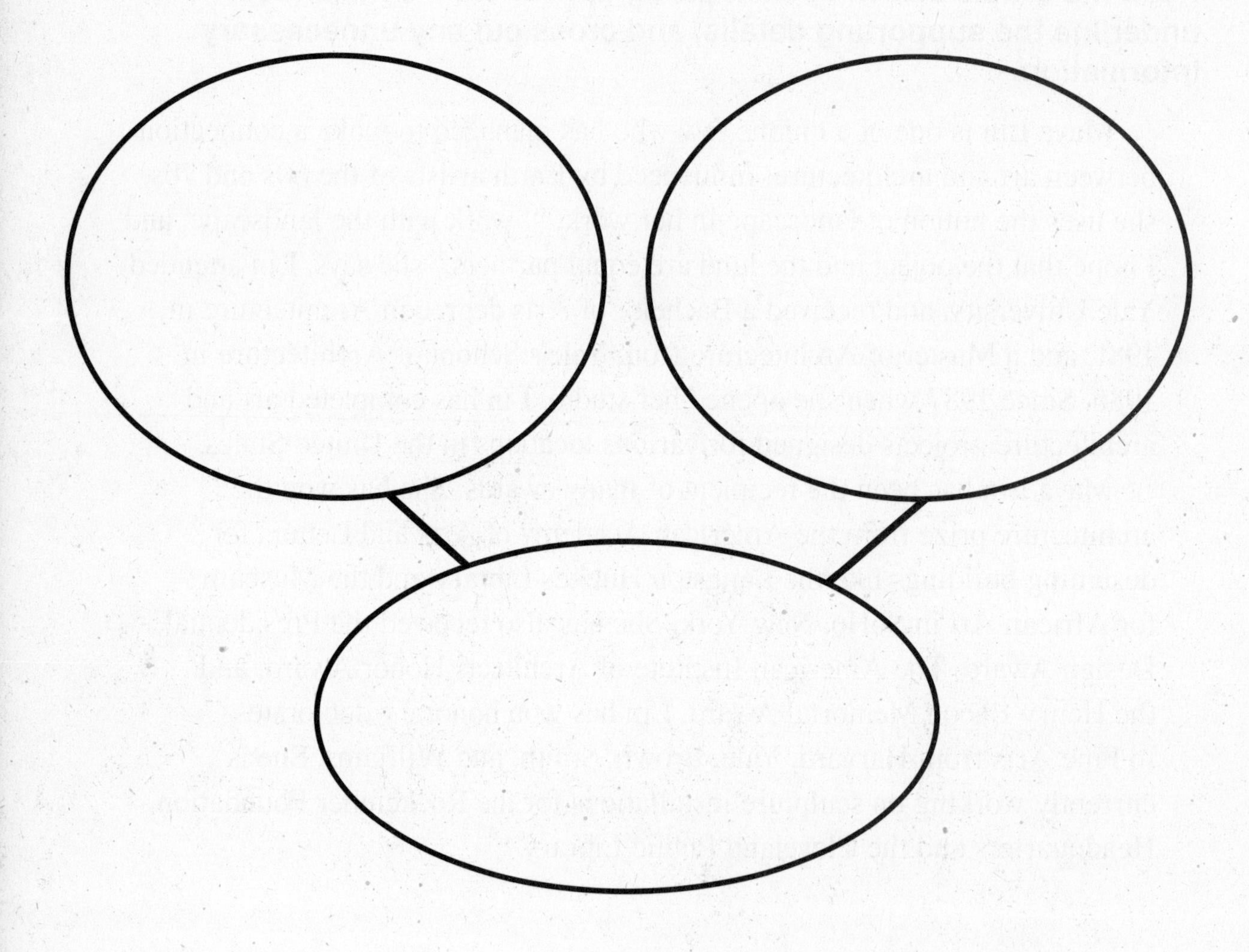

How does the information you wrote in this Main Idea Web help you summarize "Maya Lin: Architect of Memory"?

At Home: Have the student use the chart to retell the story.

Name ______________________________

As I read, I will pay attention to pronunciation.

	In 2000 the Erie Canal celebrated its 175th anniversary.
9	Today the canal is part of the New York State Canal System.
21	Visitors can explore canal museums, their **exhibits**, and
29	early boater **artifacts** in many of the major towns along the
40	canal route. In some places the once busy towpaths are now
51	pleasant bike and walking trails.
56	The best way to experience the canal is by boat. Boats
67	up to 300 feet long and 40 feet wide are welcome. Since
79	the low bridges are still around, boat height should be no
90	more than 15 to 20 feet, depending on what part of the canal
103	you explore.
105	It's also possible to travel the Erie Canal on the tugboat
116	*Urger*. The *Urger* was built in 1901 in Michigan. For the first
128	20 years of her life she was a fishing boat. Then she was sold
142	and began work as a cargo boat on the Erie Canal. She
154	continued working for about 60 years before being retired in
164	the 1980s.
166	In 1991, *Urger* was taken out of retirement. 174

Comprehension Check

1. What changes have taken place along the canal route? **Compare and Contrast**

2. What is the *Urger*? **Main Idea and Details**

	Words Read	–	Number of Errors	=	Words Correct Score
First Read		–		=	
Second Read		–		=	

At Home: Help the student read the passage, paying attention to the goal at the top of the page.

Name ______________________________

To find more information about the past, you can use the **Internet.** The Internet is made up of millions of computers that are connected to make a world wide network. You can use a search engine to find articles, images, and databases about almost any topic.

Most search engines have a system of locating specific Web sites by using key words linked by AND, OR, or NOT.

You can narrow your search by typing in key words; for example "monuments" AND "civil rights" OR "Native Americans" NOT veterans. When you want to search for words together, place them inside quotation marks. Different search engines will produce different Web page results.

Answer the following questions about the internet

1. What could you type to find information about the Vietnam Veterans Memorial Wall that Maya Lin designed? ______________________________

____

2. What could you type to find information about Sarah Salter or Willie Edwards? ______________________________

____

3. What could you type to find information about Dr. Martin Luther King Jr., but not the schools that have been named after him ______________________________

____

4. Why is it good to use more than one search engines when you are researching a topic? ______________________________

____

____

At Home: Make a list of key words to type into a search engine to find information about the Statue of Liberty.

Name ______________________________

You can add *-ed* to verbs to show that something happened in the past. You can add *-ing* to verbs to show that something is happening in the present.

Remember these spelling rules:

1. If the base word ends with a consonant, double the final consonant before adding *-ed* or *-ing.*
2. If the base word ends in *y,* change the *y* to *i* before adding *-ed* or *-ing.*
3. If the base word ends in silent **e**, drop the **e** before adding *-ed* or *-ing.*

A. Fill in the chart below.

Base Word	add *-ed*	add *-ing*
drip		
rake		
dedicate		
rely		
refer		

B. Now write a paragraph about a monument that you would like to design. Use three words with inflected endings.

____

____

____

____

____

____

At Home: Read a newspaper, and find four examples of words with inflected endings.

Name ______________________________

The **inflected endings** -*ed* and -*ing* are added to a word to show a change in the way the word is used. When you add an inflected ending, follow the spelling rules shown in the examples below to keep the vowel sound of the base word the same.

Read these examples:

hope + -***ing*** = hoping	Drop the silent **e** so that ***hope*** keeps a long ***o*** sound.
hop + -***ing*** = hopping	Double the end consonant so that ***hop*** keeps a short ***o*** sound.
deny + -***ed*** = denied	Change the ***y*** to ***i*** so that ***deny*** keeps the long **e** sound and the long ***i*** sound of ***y***.

Suppose that you are planning to visit Muir Woods National Monument in California. Write a letter with questions and ideas about your trip to a park ranger at Muir Woods on the lines below. Use six words with inflected endings in your letter.

____

____

____

____

____

____

____

____

____

____

____

____

At Home: List five words that can end in either ***-ed*** or ***-ing***. Write your own dictionary entries for the five words.

Name ______________________

Think about the meaning of each boldfaced vocabulary word. Then write a sentence containing that word. Make sure your sentence shows that you know the definition of the vocabulary word.

1. **forbidden** ______________________

2. **reluctant** ______________________

3. **mischievous** ______________________

4. **hesitation** ______________________

5. **blared** ______________________

6. **gossiped** ______________________

7. **elegant** ______________________

8. **irresistible** ______________________

Name ______________________________

Identifying a story character's **problem** and paying attention to how that character finds a **solution** will help you better understand the story.

Read the story below. Then answer the questions.

Kaitlin put her food tray on the table, looked at her watch, and said, "Ten minutes to eat again!" Janell, mumbled between bites of her sandwich, "What else is new?"

Tearing through the sandwich wrapper, Kaitlin felt angry. It wasn't fair that the line was always so long. There had to be something she could do to change things. Kaitlin looked around and counted three workers in the cafeteria. Millie was at the cash register and Alice and Mo were behind the counter dishing out the casserole even though most kids ordered cold sandwiches on Fridays. Suddenly Kaitlin said. "I'm going to write a letter to Mrs. Bromley," she exclaimed.

Janell gasped, "The principal? Kaitlin, are you serious?"

"I certainly am," Kaitlin answered. "I don't know how much money the school has, but I hope there's enough for another cash register."

1. Who is the main character in the story?

____

2. What problem does the main character have?

____

____

3. What solution does the main character come up with?

____

____

4. What will the rest of the story probably be about?

____

____

At Home: Think about a problem at your school. Try to think of more than one possible solution.

Name ______________________________

As you read *The Night of San Juan,* fill in the Story Map.

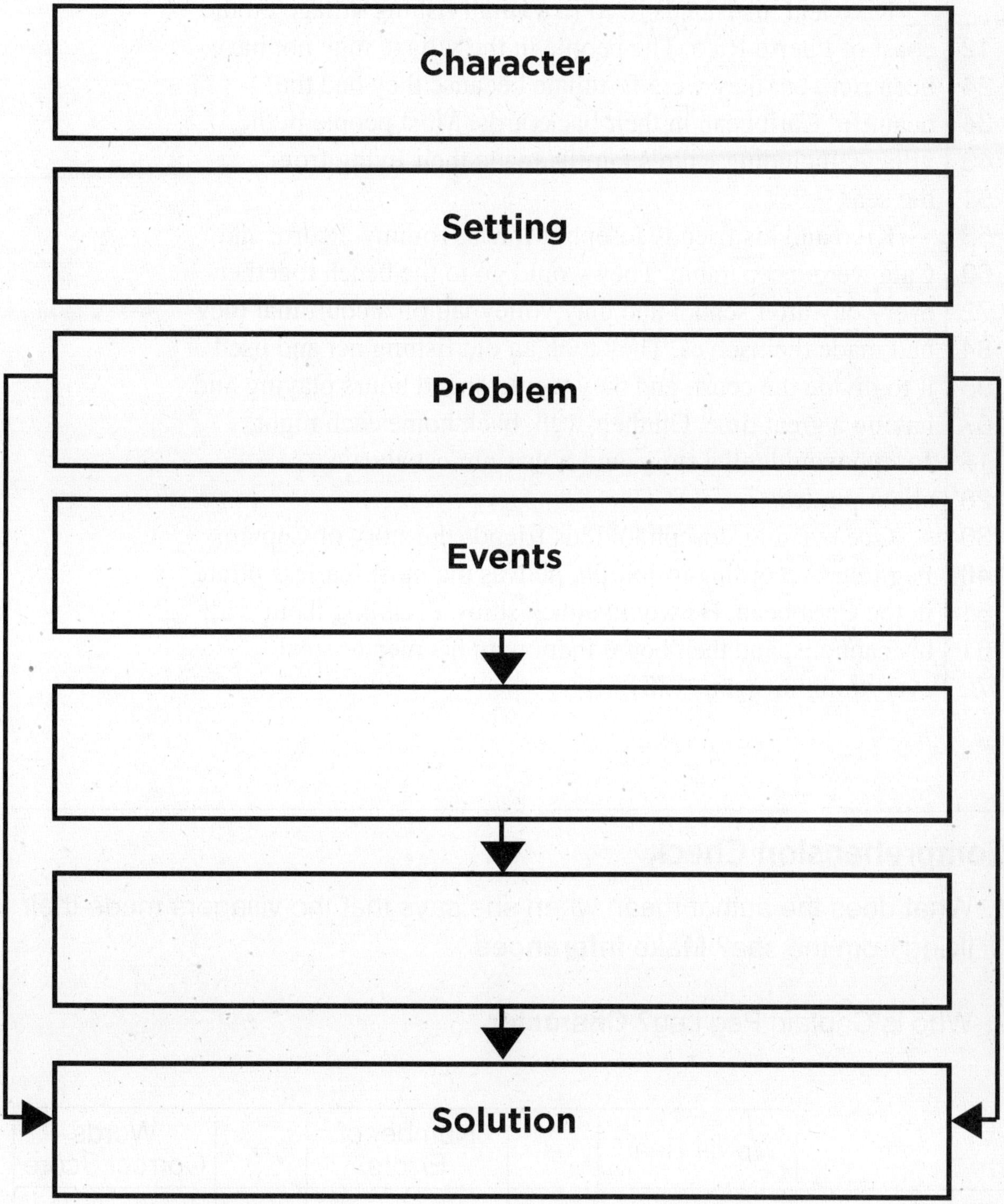

Character

Setting

Problem

Events

Solution

How does the information you wrote in the Story Map help you summarize *The Night of San Juan*?

At Home: Have the student use the chart to retell the story.

Name ______________________________

As I read, I will pay attention to pauses and intonation.

Kiko and his friends lived in a small fishing village on the
12 coast of Puerto Rico. The people in the village may not have
24 been rich, but they were fortunate because they had the
34 beautiful Caribbean in their backyards. Most people in the
43 village, including Kiko's family, made their living from
51 the sea.
53 Kiko and his friends Joseph, Morris, Tommy, Pedro, and
62 Cala were inseparable. They would go to the beach together
72 every day after school and play volleyball on a court that they
84 had made themselves. They took an old fishing net and used
95 it to divide the court, and they would spend hours playing and
107 having a great time. On their walk back home each night,
118 Joseph would tell a story, and it was almost always
128 about pirates.
130 One evening, Joseph told his friends the story of Captain
140 Peg Leg. According to Joseph, he was the most fearless pirate
151 in the Caribbean. He would attack ships, disabling them with
161 his cannons, and then board them with his men to steal
172 everything in sight. 175

Comprehension Check

1. What does the author mean when she says that the villagers made their living from the sea? **Make Inferences**

2. Who is Captain Peg Leg? **Character**

	Words Read	–	Number of Errors	=	Words Correct Score
First Read		–		=	
Second Read		–		=	

At Home: Help the student read the passage, paying attention to the goal at the top of the page.

Name ______________________________

An almanac is a reference book that is published each year. Almanac entries provide brief facts and statistics about a topic. The information is presented in a **chart**.

Look at the chart about Puerto Rico below. Use the information in the chart to fill in the blanks of the passage below.

Commonwealth of Puerto Rico

Population (2003): 3,885,877
Official languages: Spanish and English
Total land area: 3,425 square miles
Capital: San Juan
Climate: mild, with an average temperature of 77°F
Chief crops: coffee, plantains, pineapples, tomatoes, sugarcane, bananas, mangoes
Flower: Flor de maga (Puerto Rican hibiscus)
Tree: Ceiba
Bird: Reina mora

We spent today walking around ________________, the capital of Puerto Rico. We hear people speaking in __________________________ as both are official languages. In the marketplace, we see

____

____, for all these crops are grown here on the island. There is also a beautiful hibiscus flower called ________________. All these plants can grow year round because the climate is ____.

At Home: Make up a name of a country. Write a chart for an imaginary country. Use the example above as a model.

Name ______________________________

Suffixes are word parts added to the ends of base words to change their meanings or their parts of speech.

- The suffix **-ity** means "the state of."
- The suffix **-ion** means "act or process."
- The suffix **-ous** means "having the qualities of."

Word	Suffix	New Word	New Meaning
visible	-ity	visibility	the state of being visible
demonstrate	-ion	demonstration	the act of demonstrating
poison	-ous	poisonous	having the qualities of poison

Use the suffixes *-ity, -ion,* and *-ous* to change the meaning of each word below. Then write a sentence that contains the new word. Remember that there may be spelling changes when you add the suffix.

1. mischief ____________________

____

____

2. glory ____________________

____

3. humid ____________________

____

____

4. instruct ____________________

____

____

At Home: Think of two more words that end with each suffix. Identify the base of each of these words.

Name ____

- The /ô/ sound can be spelled **aw,** as in **law, ough** as in **thought,** or **au,** as in **haul.**
- The /**ou**/ sound can be spelled **ou,** as in **counter,** or **ow,** as in **cow.**
- The /**oi**/ sound can be spelled **oi,** as in **boil,** or **oy,** as in **loyal.**

A. Fill in each column of the chart with five words that have either the /ô/, the /ou/, or the /oi/ sound. Make sure that each column contains words that spell the sound differently.

/ô/ in law, haul, thought	/ou/ in counter, cow	/oi/ in boil, loyal

B. Use your completed chart to write the ways to spell each sound.

1. words with /ô/ ____

2. words with /ou/ ____

3. words with /oi/ ____

C. Complete the sentences by using a word that has the *ou* sound.

4. When my uncle goes to the diner he likes to sit at the ______________.

5. People throw coins in a ______________ for good luck.

6. You must lay a ______________ before you erect a building.

At Home: With a family member or helper, think of two additional words that fit each sound.

Name ______________________________

Read each partial sentence. Think about the meaning of the underlined vocabulary word. Then complete each sentence to show that you know the meaning of that word.

1. As the sun sets, the horizon ______________________________
____

2. If a cowboy's horse swerved suddenly while galloping, ______________________________
____

3. When the light flickered, ______________________________
____

4. The vastness of the open plains makes many people ______________________________
____

5. If something is suspended from a saddle, ______________________________
____

6. A cowboy might show enthusiasm for a task ______________________________
____

7. For many cowboys, the presence of so many cattle ______________________________
____

8. An area that has a ravine ______________________________
____

Name ____________________

An inference is a conclusion or deduction made from evidence. You **make inferences** about story elements from details in the story or from your own experience. You can combine what you already know with what you read.

Read each sentence and think about what it states. Then write one inference that you can make from that sentence.

1. Although the former slave could not read, he was the only one who could track a herd of wild horses and bring it in alone.

____

____

2. A wild horse smells smoke from miles away and begins to pace about nervously.

____

____

3. When lightning flashes, a horse rears up and then races away in the opposite direction.

____

4. Many hoofprints can be found on one side of the river, but none on the other side.

____

____

5. When a horse hears a rattlesnake, it snorts and moves away quickly.

____

6. A herd's leader constantly listens for strange sounds and sniffs the air.

____

____

At Home: Write an advertisement for a cowboy who can bring in a herd of horses single-handedly.

Name ___________________________________

As you read *Black Cowboy, Wild Horses,* fill in the Inferences Chart.

Text Clues	What You Know	Inferences

How does the information you wrote in the Inferences Chart help you monitor comprehension of *Black Cowboy, Wild Horses*?

At Home: Have the student use the chart to retell the story.

Name ______________________________

As I read, I will pay attention to expression, phrasing, and tempo.

	William F. Cody was born in Iowa in 1846. His father
11	was killed when he was just 11, and within a year, the boy
24	had a job. He worked as a cattle driver for a wagon train.
37	When he was just 13, he joined the Colorado Gold Rush. At
49	15, he was a rider for the Pony Express.
58	The Pony Express delivered mail. It used riders and
67	teams of horses to carry mail across the West. In its day, it
80	was the fastest way to bring mail to California. It helped link
92	that area to the rest of the country.
100	Cody worked hard. On one trip, he covered 300 miles
110	(483 km) in less than a day. He changed horses 20 times
121	because the horses got tired out from running. This story
131	was the first of many that added to the legend of Buffalo Bill.
144	The telegraph put an end to the Pony Express. Fast as its
156	riders were, telegrams were even faster. Still, people told
165	many stories about the Pony Express. Its riders were seen as
176	brave and daring. 179

Comprehension Check

1. What is the Pony Express? **Summarize**
2. How did the invention of the telegraph affect the Pony Express? **Cause and Effect**

	Words Read	–	Number of Errors	=	Words Correct Score
First Read		–		=	
Second Read		–		=	

At Home: Help the student read the passage, paying attention to the goal at the top of the page.

Name ___________________________

Many poems contain **repetition.** Repetition means some element is repeated, either words or lines. **Assonance** is the repetition of the same or similar vowel sounds in a series of words.

Read the poem. Then answer the questions.

1 Now, boys. Get down from your bunks, boys.
2 Strap on your hats and your chaps, boys.
3 Strap on those saddles and scat, boys.

4 Now, boys. Get down from your bunks, boys.
5 Scoop up your spurs and your boots, boys.
6 Loop up your lassoes and shoo, boys.

7 Oh, you know how, boys. . . .
8 You're cowboys!

1. Where do you see repetition? ___________________________
2. Where is assonance in the repeated lines? ___________________________
3. Why isn't *boys* an example of assonance? ___________________________
4. Where is assonance in line 2? ___________________________
5. Where is assonance in line 3? ___________________________
6. Where is assonance in line 5? ___________________________
7. Where is assonance in line 6? ___________________________
8. Is there assonance in line 7? ___________________________

At Home: Use another poem that has repetition and assonance. Write down the words, underlining the lines and vowel sounds that repeat.

Name ______________________________

Analogies are a way of showing relationships between pairs of words. Analogies contain two pairs of words, and both pairs have the same relationship. If the words in the first pair are **antonyms,** then the words in the second pair should also be antonyms.

hollow	fragment	flickered	vast	mutter
right	gallop	presence	complicated	valley

Complete each of the analogies below with a word from the box.

1. **Sun** is to **shade** as **limited** is to ______________
2. **Lost** is to **found** as **dense** is to ______________
3. **Few** is to **many** as **mountain** is to ______________
4. **Sit** is to **stand** as **trot** is to ______________
5. **Obvious** is to **invisible** as **whole** is to ______________
6. **Generous** is to **stingy** as **shout** is to ______________
7. **Darkness** is to **light** as **absence** is to ______________
8. **Formal** is to **casual** as **continuous** is to ______________
9. **Bottom** is to **top** as **left** is to ______________
10. **Straight** is to **crooked** as **simple** is to ______________

At Home: Make up and write down three of your own analogies using pairs of antonyms. Ask a family member to solve them.

Name ______________________________

Practice

Phonics: VCCV Pattern

Recognizing syllables can help you read and spell. Some syllables end with vowels and others end with consonants. If a word contains a **Vowel-Consonant-Consonant-Vowel (VCCV) pattern,** the first vowel sound is usually short. Divide VCCV words into syllables between the two consonants. This is true whether the two consonants are the same, forming a doublet, or whether they are different.

Say the words below to yourself, and listen to each syllable. Then write the words in the correct column of the chart. Draw a line between the syllables. Add two more words to each column.

mutter	hollow	pigment	empire
dentist	mustang	gallop	jogger
fragment	kennel	vulture	flatter

VCCV with Doublet	VCCV Pattern with Different Consonants

At Home: Find words that contain the VCCV pattern in a magazine or newspaper.

Name ______________________________

sympathy	alert	dedicated	blared	presence
predators	slurp	irresistible	swerved	equality

A. Choose the word from the box above that best completes each sentence.

1. The dog was so cute and friendly that he was simply ______________.
2. The hikers were ______________ after a rattlesnake was seen on the trail.
3. Archaeologists are ______________ to uncovering the past.
4. The girls had ______________ for their friend, who couldn't play outside.
5. Some snakes are dangerous ______________ that kill their prey.
6. ______________ means equal and fair treatment before the law for everyone.

ravine	species	site	shrieks	injury	hesitation

B. Write a story about a character who encounters an animal. Use at least five of the six words in the box above.

____

____

____

____

____

____

____

____

Name ____________________

Read each clue. Write the matching vocabulary word on the line next to it. Then use the word correctly in a sentence on the line below.

vibrates	enthusiasm	suspended	vastness
reluctant	bulletin board	artifacts	forbidden

1. shakes quickly ____________

____

____

2. unwilling ____________

____

____

3. intense excitement ____________

____

____

4. objects or parts of objects left by past civilizations ____________

____

____

5. a place for posting notices, announcements, and pictures ____________

____

____

6. not allowed or off limits ____________

____

____

Name ______________________________

Read each clue below to complete the crossword puzzle.

Across

2. to walk in a way that is too proud

3. empty, bare

5. leader or ruler of a state, usually elected

8. to teach

Down

1. steering a ship on its course

4. ruler who rules unjustly

6. people who are loyal to a nation

7. spirit, liveliness

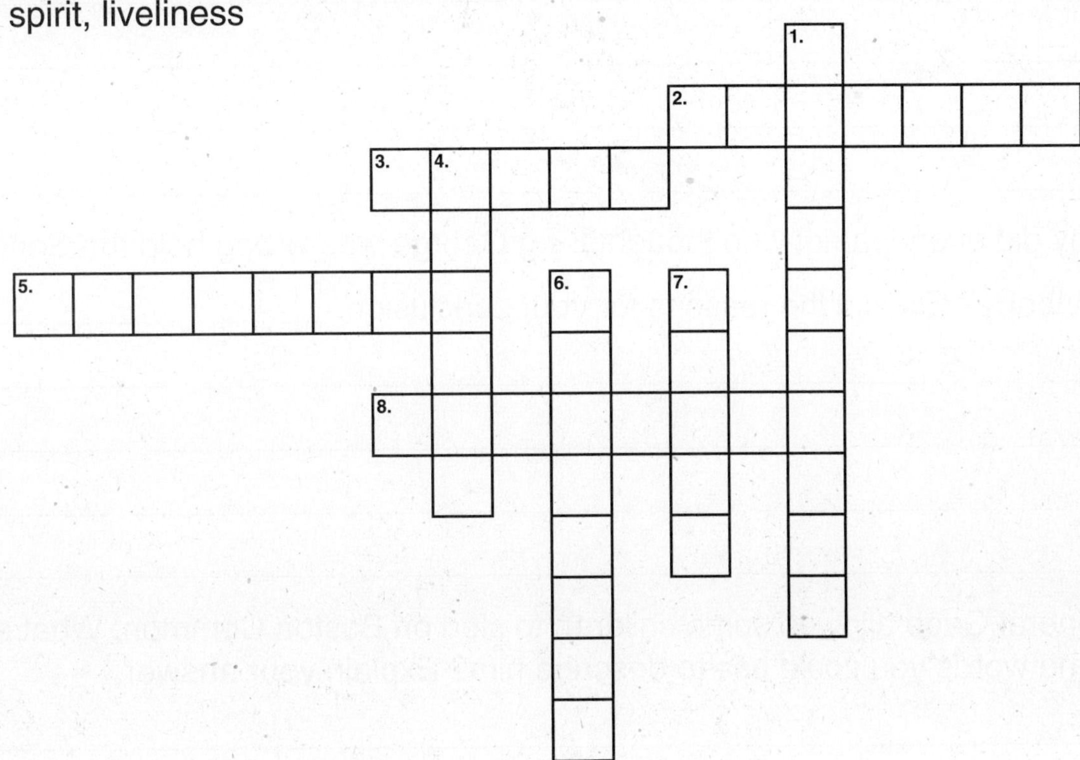

Name ______________________________

Use information from your own knowledge to draw conclusions about the following questions.

1. How do the people of Boston feel about having the British soldiers on their Common? Explain the reasons for your conclusion.

____

____

____

____

2. Why would someone tell his children to listen with their eyes and ears when they go to the Common? Explain your answer. ______________________________

____

____

____

____

3. Why did every patriot who thought King George was wrong help the Sons of Liberty? Explain the reasons for your conclusion. ______________________________

____

____

____

____

4. General Gage allowed some children to sled on Boston Common. What are some words you could use to describe him? Explain your answer.

____

____

____

____

At Home: Ask a family member to find a family photograph from the past. Draw a conclusion about the people, place, or time shown in the photograph.

Name ______________________________

As you read *Sleds on Boston Common,* fill in the Conclusions Chart.

Text Clues	Conclusion

How does the information you wrote in the Conclusions Chart help you make inferences and analyze *Sleds on Boston Common*?

At Home: Have the student use the chart to retell the story.

Name ______________________________

As I read, I will pay attention to pauses.

	Boston became the center of colonial protests against the
9	British. Samuel Adams and other **Patriots** called King George III
18	a **tyrant**. In 1770, British troops killed six people in a riot known
30	as the Boston Massacre. In 1773 during the Boston Tea Party,
40	Patriots threw British tea into the harbor. They were protesting a
51	tax they viewed as unfair. King George III had seen enough. He
62	thought what was happening in the colonies was a **stark** case of
74	rebellion. It was time to get tough.
81	The British governor of Massachusetts in 1775 was General
89	Thomas Gage. To stop the colonists' rebellion, Gage had orders
99	to arrest two Patriot leaders, Sam Adams and John Hancock.
109	When British spies had found out that Hancock and Adams were
120	hiding in the village of Lexington near Boston, Gage decided to act.
132	The spies also told Gage that the Patriot militia, a group of colonists
145	ready to fight, was in nearby Concord. This group, called the
156	Minutemen, had hidden guns and gunpowder there.
163	The Patriots also had spies. They found out the British plans. 174

Comprehension Check

1. What caused the Boston Tea Party? **Cause and Effect**

2. How did the British and the Patriots find out information about each other? **Main Idea and Details**

	Words Read	–	Number of Errors	=	Words Correct Score
First Read		–		=	
Second Read		–		=	

At Home: Help the student read the passage, paying attention to the goal at the top of the page.

Meter is the regular arrangement of accented and unaccented syllables in a line of poetry. **Alliteration** is the repetition of the same first letter or sound in a series of words.

A. Write a poem about the American Revolution that uses meter and alliteration.

____

____

____

____

____

____

____

____

____

____

____

____

____

____

____

____

____

____

____

At Home: Identify the use of alliteration in your poem.

Name ______________________________

A *prefix* is a word part that is added to the beginning of a base word and changes its meaning. A *suffix* is a word part that is added to the end of a base word and changes its meaning.

A. Read the prefixes and suffixes shown in the chart. Use these prefixes and suffixes to write words in each word family. Check your answers in a dictionary.

Prefix	Meaning
dis-	the opposite of
un-	not

Suffix	Meaning
-ic	having
-ism	act of or state of
-ful	full of

Trust **Word Family**

1. ______________
2. ______________
3. ______________

Belief **Word Family**

4. ______________

Patriot **Word Family**

5. ______________
6. ______________
7. ______________

Truth **Word Family**

8. ______________
9. ______________
10. ______________

B. Make a new word family for another word.

11. ______________
12. ______________
13. ______________

At Home: Work with a family member or helper to make word families for *color*, *real*, and *grace*.

Name ______________________________

The point at which two syllables meet can help you decide whether the vowel sound is long or short. If the syllable ends in a vowel (as in *lo/cal*), then the vowel sound is long. If the syllable ends in a consonant (as in *sal/ad*), then the vowel sound is short.

Say the words below. Listen to the first vowel. Draw a line (/) to divide each word into syllables. Circle the word in each word pair that has the same vowel sound and syllable pattern.

Example: local ___lo/cal___ (total) salad

1. humid ______________ rumor linen
2. recent ______________ finish meter
3. closet ______________ robin minus
4. lilac ______________ shiver tiger
5. basic ______________ vacant comet
6. prison ______________ limit student
7. body ______________ legal modern
8. relish ______________ lemon labor
9. cabin ______________ decent rapid
10. punish ______________ cover tyrant
11. native ______________ dated camel
12. given ______________ favor river

At Home: Write all the words from the list on index cards. Cut the words apart after the first syllable. Mix up the cards and see who can put the most words back together again.

Name ______________________________

Use your knowledge of the *boldfaced* vocabulary words to answer each question, using a complete sentence. Use the boldfaced word in your answer.

1. What is an example of something you might **submit** to a teacher?

____

2. What is one job a **colonel** might do? ______________________________

____

3. Where might you find an **attorney?** ______________________________

____

4. If you **postpone** an event, when does it take place? ______________________________

____

5. What is one way that a person might **qualify** to vote? ______________________________

____

6. What kind of work is done by a **legislature**? ______________________________

____

7. What is one responsibility of a **representative**? ______________________________

____

8. What is an example of a **satisfactory** voting law? ______________________________

____

Name ______________________________

Facts are statements that can be proven true. **Opinions** are statements about what a person believes or prefers.

A. Read each sentence. Write *Fact* if it states a fact. Write *Opinion* if it states an opinion.

1. Esther Morris was a very brave and daring woman. ______________
2. Esther Morris was the first female in the United States to hold public office. ______________
3. Being a judge is a very difficult job. ______________
4. Wyoming was the first place in the United States to give women the right to vote. ______________

B. Underline the statements below that are facts.

5. Gold fever brought many people to the Wyoming Territory.
6. In the days of Esther Morris, Wyoming had wide, open spaces.
7. Wyoming was the best place to live in North America.
8. After 1869, women had the right to vote in Wyoming.

C. Write a paragraph about whether you would have liked living in the Wyoming Territory as it was when Esther Morris lived there.

____

____

____

____

____

At Home: Work with a family member or helper to make a list of facts and opinions about your home or neighborhood.

Name ____

As you read *When Esther Morris Headed West*, fill in the Fact and Opinion Chart.

Fact	Opinion

How does the information you wrote in the Fact and Opinion Chart help you evaluate *When Esther Morris Headed West*?

At Home: Have the student use the chart to retell the story.

Name ____________________

As I read, I will pay attention to pronunciation.

	"Free at last!" shouted the African Americans after the Civil War.
11	And that was true in many ways. They were not enslaved
22	anymore, they could live in new places, and they could
32	make some choices.
35	In our nation's capital, lawmakers were busy. They
43	passed three important changes to the Constitution, called
51	amendments. The Thirteenth Amendment ended slavery.
57	The Fourteenth Amendment gave African Americans their
64	citizenship. The Fifteenth Amendment gave all African
71	American men the right to vote.
77	But this was not an easy time for our nation. The North
89	and South still had very different opinions. Northerners
97	had won the war. They wanted changes to take place right
108	away. Some even believed the South should be punished for
118	supporting slavery and for fighting the other states.
126	The South argued that the North wanted too much change
136	too soon. 138

Comprehension Check

1. What did our nation's lawmakers do for African Americans? **Main Idea and Details**
2. How did the North and South feel at the end of the Civil War? **Compare and Contrast**

	Words Read	–	Number of Errors	=	Words Correct Score
First Read		–		=	

At Home: Help the student read the passage, paying attention to the goal at the top of the page.

Name ______________________________

A **time line** is a diagram of several events arranged in the order in which they took place. A time line helps to organize information in an easy, visual way.

A. Look at the time line and answer the questions.

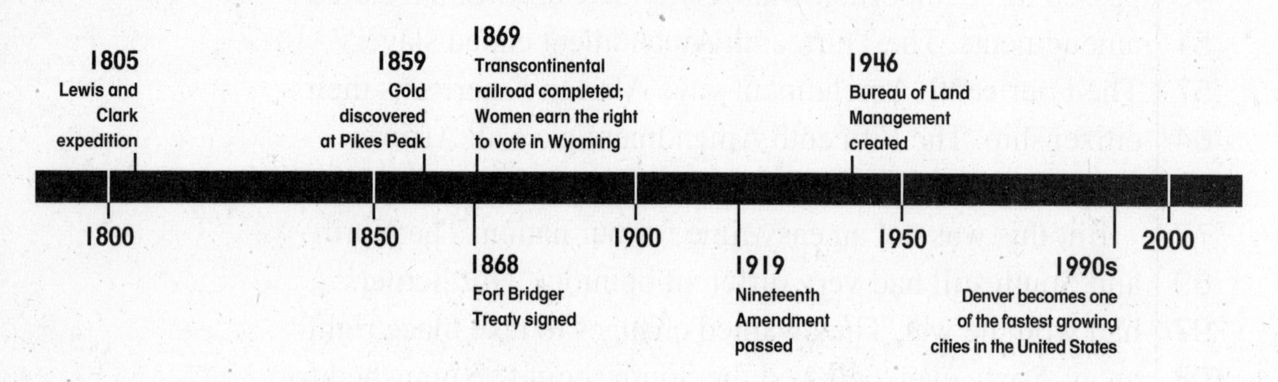

1. How many years make up this time line?

____

2. Was the railroad completed before or after Lewis and Clark's expedition? How do you know?

____

____

3. How many years before the Nineteenth Amendment was passed did women in Wyoming have the right to vote?

____

4. Where does your birthday fit on this time line?

____

B. Write a summary about the information on this time line.

____

____

____

At Home: Find a timeline in a magazine and write a summary about it.

Name ____________________________

To find out how a word is pronounced, look in a dictionary. The pronunciation, written in symbols, appears right after the entry word. To find out how to pronounce these symbols, look for the **pronunciation key**. In many dictionaries, the key appears at the bottom of every other page. Read this example of a pronunciation and part of a pronunciation key.

suffrage (sə-frij) the right to vote

Pronunciation Key

\ə\ **a**way	\a\ c**a**t	\e\ l**e**t	\i\ s**i**t	\o\ h**o**t	\u\ b**u**t
\ər\ h**er**d	\ā\ m**a**ke	\ē\ n**ee**d	\ī\ t**i**me	\ō\ j**o**ke	\ū\ c**u**te

Look up the word *colonel,* and then answer the questions.

1. How does the dictionary show the vowel sound in the first syllable of *colonel?* ___________

2. Look at the pronunciation key above. What word has the same vowel sound that appears in the first syllable of *colonel?* Underline the letter or letters that stand for the sound. ___________

Look up the word *courageous,* and then answer the questions.

3. How does the dictionary show the vowel sounds in the first and last syllable of *courageous?* ___________

4. What word in the pronunciation key has the same vowel sounds that appear in the first and last syllables of *courageous?* Underline the letter or letters that stand for the sound. ___________

5. What word in the pronunciation key has the same vowel sound that appears in the second syllable of *courageous?* Underline the letter or letters that stand for the sound. ___________

At Home: Look up the word ***attorney.*** Point out the words in the pronunciation key that help you pronounce *attorney.*

Name ______________________

A. In some words, vowels that appear together are pronounced as one sound. In other words, vowels that appear together are pronounced individually. Divide each word into syllables between the vowels that appear together. Then circle the word with the same *vowel-vowel* sound.

1. poet	poem	roam
2. video	rodeo	road
3. radio	raid	patio
4. giant	diameter	maintain
5. variety	relied	science
6. riot	lion	laughter
7. actual	casual	cause
8. fuel	argued	cruel
9. genuine	ruin	bruise
10. meander	meaner	react

B. Write a paragraph about the right to vote. Use at least six V/V words. Underline each V/V word you use.

____

____

____

____

____

____

____

____

____

____

At Home: Look through newspapers and magazines to find other words that are divided into syllables between two vowels.

Practice

Vocabulary

Name ____________________

A. Use each of the words below in a sentence. Make sure that the sentence shows that you understand the meaning of the word.

1. humanity ____________________

____

2. inevitable ____________________

____

3. unheeded ____________________

____

4. enlightened ____________________

____

____

5. prevailing ____________________

____

B. Think about a problem that relates to the pollution of Earth's environment. Write a paragraph about the problem. Use each of the vocabulary words above.

____

____

____

____

____

____

____

____

____

Name ______________________________

A **fact** is something that can be proven true. An **opinion** is a belief that cannot be proven.

A. Read each opinion. Rewrite the opinion so that it is a factual statement.

1. Melting ice at the North and South poles is bad. ______________

____

2. Loss of the ozone layer poses a really big problem. ______________

____

3. Burning fossil fuels is not a good way to produce energy. ______________

____

B. Read each factual statement. Rewrite the statement so that it expresses an opinion.

4. Recycling paper saves trees and water. ______________

____

____

5. Americans throw away 65 million aluminum cans a year. ______________

____

____

6. Recycling glass helps to save electricity. ______________

____

____

At Home: Find three statements in a newspaper that are facts. Rewrite a statements so that they express opinions.

Name ____________________

As you read "Beyond the Horizon", fill in the Fact and Opinion Chart.

Opinion	
Fact	

How does the information you wrote in this Fact and Opinion Chart help you evaluate "Beyond the Horizon"?

At Home: Have the student use the chart to retell the story.

Name ________________________________

As I read, I will pay attention to pauses.

	People who are concerned about the environment often
8	look at organic farming as an enlightened way of growing
18	food. They argue that organic foods are healthier than
27	conventionally grown food because they contain fewer
34	chemicals.
35	Other people like the fact that organic farming is usually
45	done on small farms. They like knowing the people who
55	produce their food.
58	There are plenty of critics of organic farming, too.
67	Some argue that its methods can't produce enough food
76	to feed all of humanity.
81	Others point out that prevailing farming methods take
89	less land than organic farming. As a result, we're able to
100	conserve more wild lands.
104	Still, organic farming keeps growing in popularity. Even
112	agribusinesses are starting to look at it. It's clear that the older
124	way of doing things has a bright future ahead of it. 135

Comprehension Check

1. What do people say who support organic farming? **Summarize**

2. What do critics of organic farming say? **Summarize**

	Words Read	–	Number of Errors	=	Words Correct Score
First Read		–		=	
Second Read		–		=	

At Home: Help the student read the passage, paying attention to the goal at the top of the page.

Name ______________________________

There are different ways to read a nonfiction book or article. Skimming is quickly looking over a passage to identify main ideas. Scanning is searching for key words as you look over text. As you read, take notes to help you remember main ideas, names, or key words. Another method of taking notes is to write an outline, or a summary that lists the most important ideas and details of a selection.

Read the passage below, and then answer the questions.

Global warming, or the steady rising of Earth's surface temperature, results from a phenomenon called the greenhouse effect. To understand this phenomenon, think of a greenhouse. Inside the greenhouse everything stays warm. That is because the walls and ceiling of the greenhouse trap the air inside. Earth's atmosphere, the layer of gases surrounding Earth, acts like the walls and ceiling of a greenhouse. That is, the atmosphere traps heat. One gas that traps heat is carbon dioxide. Burning fossil fuels results in the release of increased carbon dioxide into the atmosphere.

If global warming continues, scientists fear that it will have dangerous consequences for Earth's environment. The ice at the North and South poles will melt if people do not take steps to stop global warming. This would cause ocean levels to rise and coastlines to flood. Furthermore, Earth's weather patterns could change, resulting in more storms, heat waves, and droughts.

1. Scan this passage for a key word or phrase. Define the term.

Key word: ______________________________

Definition: ______________________________

2. Skim this passage. What is the main idea? ______________________________

____

3. What are two notes you might take on this passage? ______________________________

____

____

At Home: Write an outline of the passage.

Name ______________________________

A **prefix** is a word part that is added to the beginning of a word. A prefix can change the meaning of a word. The prefix *un-* means *not.* The prefix *en-* means *in, put into or upon,* or *make into or make like.*

Look at each sentence, and find the word in each sentence that contains a prefix. On the line provided, write the word and its meaning. Then write your own sentence using the word.

1. Sometimes warnings go unheeded.

   Word and Meaning: ______________________________

   Sentence: ______________________________

   ____

2. To enlarge the parking lot, they would have to cut down trees.

   Word and Meaning: ______________________________

   Sentence: ______________________________

   ____

3. Some gardeners use compost and fertilizer to enrich the soil.

   Word and Meaning: ______________________________

   ____

   Sentence: ______________________________

   ____

4. My neighbor is unaware of the problem of melting ice caps.

   Word and Meaning: ______________________________

   Sentence: ______________________________

   ____

At Home: Think of a new word that uses each prefix. Write the meaning of each word.

Name ______________________________

When three consonants fall between two vowels in a word, the word has a **Vowel-Consonant-Consonant-Consonant-Vowel,** or **VCCCV, pattern.** To divide a word that follows the VCCCV pattern, look for consonant blends, or pairs of consonants that work together in the word to make one sound. You cannot separate a word's syllables between the two consonants of a consonant blend.

Examples of Words with the VCCCV Pattern
First Syllable Consonant Blend: trust/ful
Second Syllable Consonant Blend: dis/trust

Divide compound words between the two words that make up the compound word. For example, the word *landlord* is divided as *land/lord.* The consonant blend is in the first syllable.

A. Draw a line (/) to divide each word in the box into two syllables.

orphan	complain	endless	hurtful
harmless	impress	conflict	reckless

B. Write each word from the box in the correct column of the chart. Complete the chart with four compound words: two that have a consonant blend in the first syllable, and two that have a consonant blend in the second syllable.

First Syllable Consonant Blend	Second Syllable Consonant Blend

At Home: List four more words with a VCCCV pattern.

Name ______________________________

Write a sentence for each of the words below. Make sure that the sentences show that you understand the meaning of each word.

1. progress ______________________________

2. brimming ______________________________

3. scrawny ______________________________

4. landscape ______________________________

5. scorching ______________________________

6. parched ______________________________

7. gnarled ______________________________

8. gushed ______________________________

Name ______________________________

When you **compare** things, you tell how they are alike.
When you **contrast** things, you tell how they are different.

A. Compare and contrast a desert habitat to where you live.

____
____
____
____
____
____
____
____
____
____
____
____
____
____
____
____
____
____

B. Then, on a separate sheet of paper, make a Venn Diagram using information from your essay.

At Home: Think of an invention that changed people's lives. Compare and contrast the way people lived before and after that invention.

Name ______________________________

As you read *My Great-Grandmother's Gourd,* fill in the Venn Diagrams.

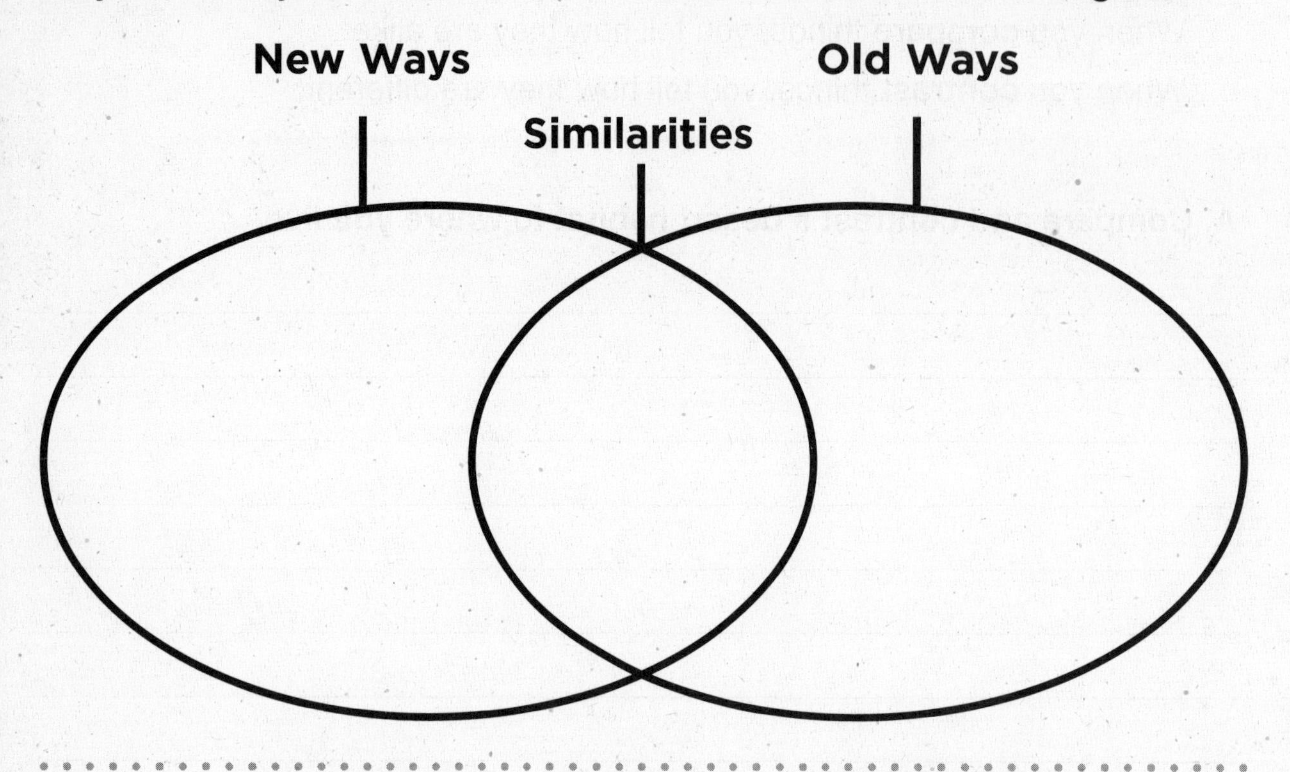

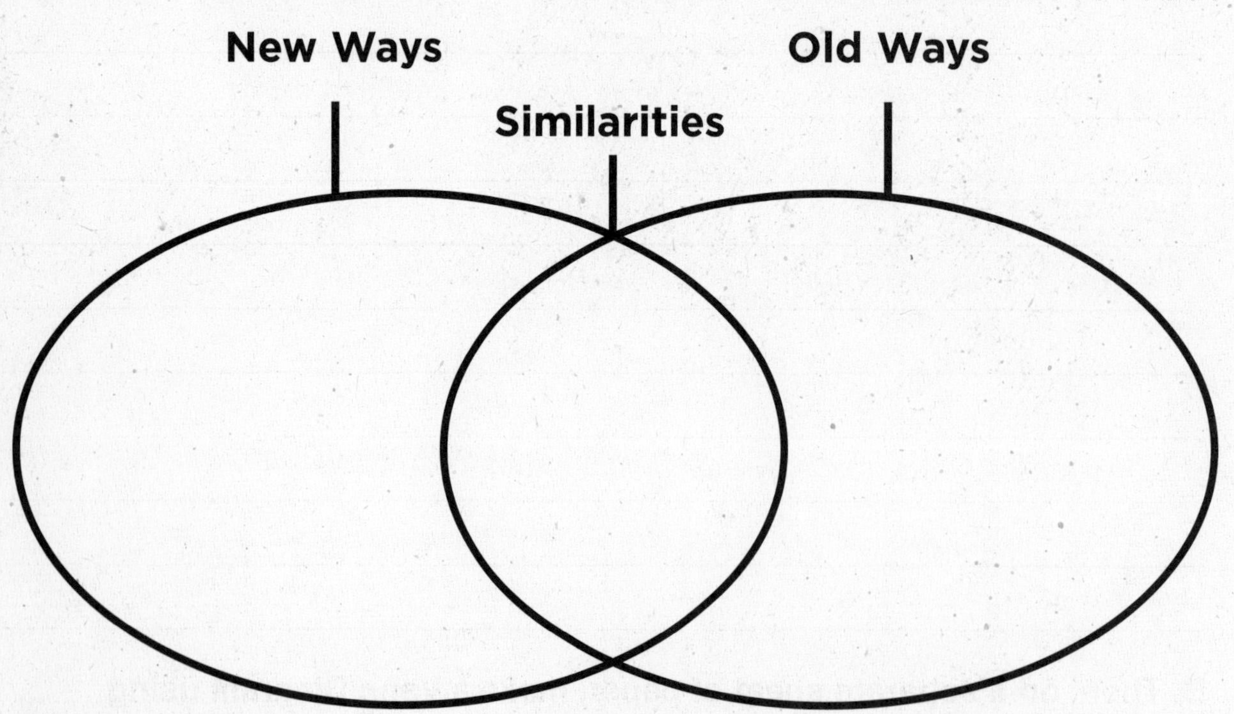

How does the information you wrote in the Venn Diagrams help you make inferences and analyze *My Great-Grandmother's Gourd*?

At Home: Have the student use the chart to retell the story

Name ______________________________

As I read, I will pay attention to tempo.

The Gobi Desert is located on the continent of
9 Asia. If you look at a map, you will see that Mongolia is
22 right in the middle of Asia. Far from any coast, ocean, or sea,
35 the area is landlocked. There is land on all sides.
45 The Gobi Desert is a continental desert that formed
54 because it lay far away from any water source and
64 surrounded by high mountains. However, only the southern
72 part of the Gobi is true desert. Flat Gobi plateau is dry and
85 barren. The rest is dry, grassy steppe, like much of the rest of
98 Mongolia. Rain and snow fall high in the mountains that
108 border the desert.
111 The Gobi Desert has extreme weather conditions. There
119 is no humidity, or moisture in the air, and the daytime sun
131 is **scorching**. The temperatures range from sub-zero in the
140 winter to summer highs around 130 degrees Fahrenheit
147 (54 degrees Celsius). Winds can bring on sudden
154 temperature changes in just a few minutes. You might be
164 gushing sweat in a T-shirt one moment and scrambling for
174 your warm hat and boots the next. 181

Comprehension Check

1. What does the word landlocked mean? **Context Clues**

2. What is the weather like in the Gobi Desert? **Summarize**

	Words Read	–	Number of Errors	=	Words Correct Score
First Read		–		=	
Second Read		–		=	

At Home: Help the student read the passage, paying attention to the goal at the top of the page.

Name ______________________________

Look at the diagram. Then answer the questions.

2. Condensation: The water vapor rises, forms clouds, and is cooled by the air.

3. Precipitation: Water returns to Earth's surface as rain, snow, or other precipitation. Some water seeps into the ground. Some water returns to the ocean.

1. Evaporation: The sun heats water in the soil, rivers, lakes, and oceans. The water evaporates and turns into water vapor, a gas.

1. What does the diagram show?

____

____

2. Why is the sun important to the water cycle?

____

____

3. What is groundwater?

____

____

4. Do you think this process diagram is helpful? Explain your answer.

____

____

____

____

At Home: Draw a process diagram that shows an everyday process in your home.

Name ______________________________

Denotation is the exact meaning of a word. Synonyms usually have denotations similar to the original word. Synonyms can also carry positive or negative impressions, or **connotations**. For example, a **strong-willed** person can be called **stubborn**, which has a negative connotation, or **determined**, which has a more positive connotation. Some words are neutral.

A. For each word below, find one synonym. Then write whether the connotation of the synonym is positive, negative, or neutral.

Word	Synonym	Connotation
plain		
work		
boastful		
immature		
serious		

B. Choose two words from the chart, and write one sentence that uses the exact meaning of the word and one sentence that uses its synonym.

1. ______________________________

____

____

____

2. ______________________________

____

____

At Home: Choose three more words from the chart above. Write sentences that use synonyms of each word.

Name ______________________________

In words that have more than one syllable, one syllable is always stressed, or accented, more than the others. A stressed syllable can appear at the beginning or at the end of a two syllable word. The unaccented syllable often has the unaccented vowel sound /ə/. For example, the second syllable of the word *confirm* is accented. The first syllable has the /ə/ sound.

Look at each word below and circle the accented syllable. Then use a dictionary to check your work and write the pronunciation on the line provided.

1. canal ______________ **4.** pronounce ______________

2. perplex ______________ **5.** venom ______________

3. lentil ______________ **6.** helpful ______________

Now find your own words that fit the pattern and do the same for each.

7. /ə/ spelled *a* : ______________ ______________

8. /ə/ spelled e : ______________ ______________

9. /ə/ spelled *i* : ______________ ______________

10. /ə/ spelled *o* : ______________ ______________

11. /ə/ spelled *o* : ______________ ______________

12. /ə/ spelled *u* : ______________ ______________

At Home: Use a dictionary to find five words with other sounds in the unaccented syllable, such as *belief* and *digest*.

Name ______________________________

Read each sentence beginning. Think about the meaning of the *boldfaced* vocabulary word. Then complete each sentence to show the meaning of that word.

1. We have programmed our **robot** to ______________________________
____
______________________________.

2. When I **reversed** the controls, ______________________________
____
______________________________.

3. Our robot **rotated** when ______________________________
____
______________________________.

4. Taking **tokens** off the gameboard ______________________________
____
______________________________.

5. Perhaps the robot **staggered** because ______________________________
____
______________________________.

6. That **defective** robot ______________________________
____
______________________________.

7. Wires were **dangling** ______________________________
____
______________________________.

8. A **meteor** can ______________________________
____
______________________________.

Name ______________________________

When you **draw conclusions,** you make a judgment or inference about something. Readers draw conclusions and so do characters in stories. Conclusions can be based on events, words, and facts given in a story, as well as on information that you already know. Characters often draw conclusions that are based on the actions of other characters.

Read the passage below and then write two separate paragraphs. Write two different conclusions you can draw about the situation that is described.

Back from her trip, Mrs. Hernandez looked out the door and gasped! The hole in the backyard, or the hole that seemed to *be* the backyard, was much larger than she had expected. She wondered again how bad it was going to be and what she was going to tell her children.

Possible conclusion 1: ______________________________

____

____

____

____

____

____

Possible conclusion 2: ______________________________

____

____

____

____

____

____

At Home: Choose a newspaper or magazine article and draw a conclusion from the piece. Provide supporting information that led you to that conclusion.

Name ______________________________

As you read *Zathura*, fill in the Conclusions Diagrams.

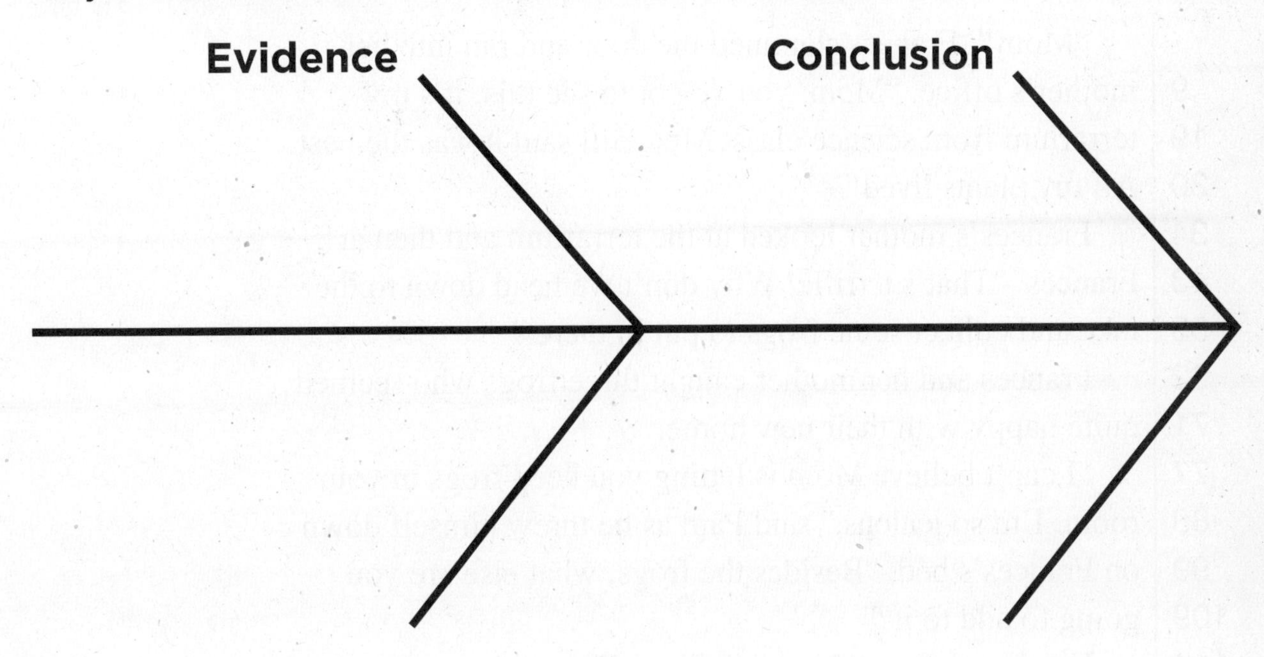

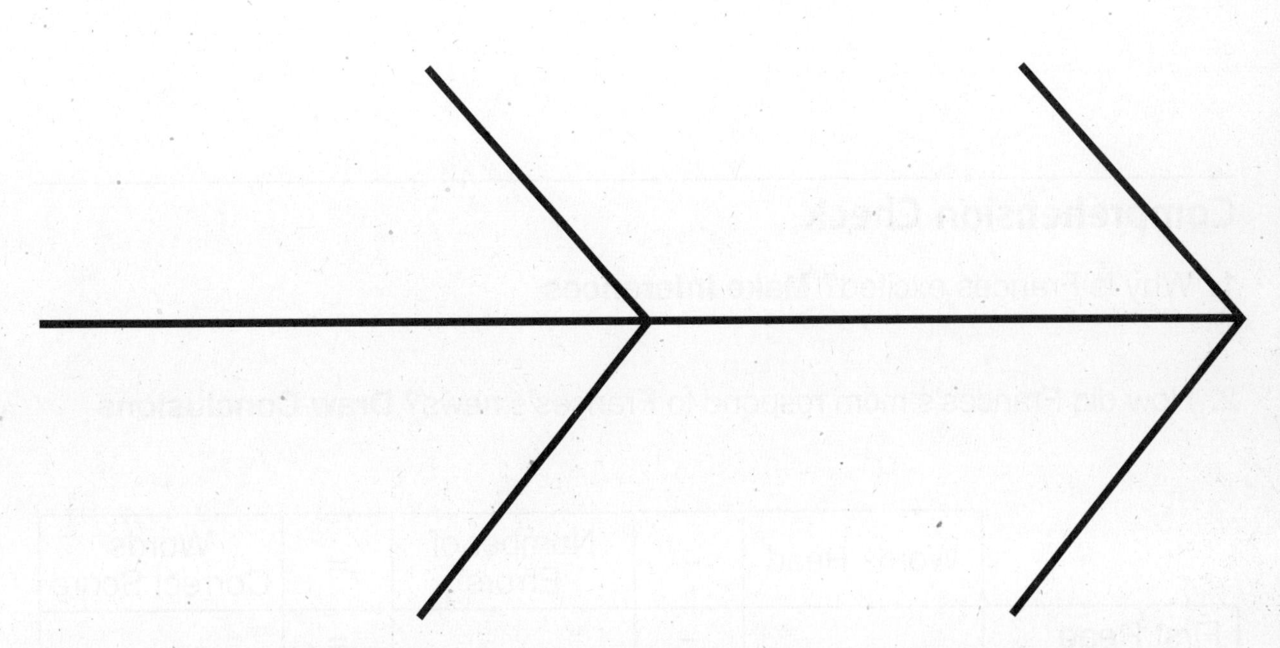

How does the information you wrote in the Conclusions Diagrams help you make inferences and analyze *Zathura*?

At Home: Have the student use the chart to retell the story.

Name ______________________________

As I read, I will pay attention to punctuation.

	“Mom!” Frances slammed the door and ran into her
9	mother’s office. “Mom, you’ve got to see this. It’s my
19	terrarium from science class. Mrs. Gill said it was the best.
30	All my plants lived!”
34	Frances’s mother looked at the terrarium and then at
43	Frances. “That’s terrific! Why don’t we head down to the
53	lake and collect some frogs to put in there.”
62	Frances and her mother caught three frogs who seemed
71	quite happy with their new home.
77	“I can’t believe Mom is letting you keep frogs in your
88	room. I’m so jealous,” said Paul as he threw himself down
99	on Frances’s bed. “Besides the frogs, what else are you
109	going to add to it?”
114	Frances was watching the frogs. “I don’t know. Maybe
123	a lizard?”
125	Paul sat up, “Let’s get our bikes and go to Mr. Peters’
137	Pets right now.” 140

Comprehension Check

1. Why is Frances excited? **Make Inferences**

2. How did Frances’s mom respond to Frances’s news? **Draw Conclusions**

	Words Read	–	Number of Errors	=	Words Correct Score
First Read		–		=	
Second Read		–		=	

At Home: Help the student read the passage, paying attention to the goal at the top of the page.

Name ______________________________

Write an article about what robots will do in the future. Be certain to include a headline and byline.

At Home: Rewrite the headlines of different newspaper or magazine articles.

Name ______________________________

Analogies show relationships. They often contain two pairs of words that show a similar relationship. If the words in the first pair are **synonyms**, then the words in the second pair should also be synonyms, as in this analogy:

Conquer is to **defeat** as **irritate** is to ______________.

To complete this analogy, you might think, "*Conquer* means the same as *defeat.* What word means the same as *irritate? Bother* is a synonym for *irritate,* so it correctly completes the analogy."

Choose a word from the list below to complete each of the following analogies.

intelligent	everyday	lessen	defective	revise
frequently	uncertain	stride	fearless	produce

1. **Increase** is to **extend** as **decrease** is to ______________.
2. **Perfect** is to **faultless** as **brave** is to ______________.
3. **Fix** is to **repair** as **rewrite** is to ______________.
4. **Grand** is to **magnificent** as **common** is to ______________.
5. **Magnificent** is to **great** as **smart** is to ______________.
6. **Run** is to **hasten** as **march** is to ______________.
7. **Ripped** is to **torn** as **flawed** is to ______________.
8. **Ruin** is to **destroy** as **make** is to ______________.
9. **Seldom** is to **rarely** as **often** is to ______________.
10. **Worthless** is to **useless** as **doubtful** is to ______________.

At Home: Using pairs of synonyms, write three analogies. Ask a family member or helper to fill in the blanks.

Name ______________________________

The /ər/ sound is often found in an unaccented syllable. The three most common spellings for words that end in the /ə/ sound + r are **-ar**, **-er**, and **-or**.

Make three columns, one for words ending in *-ar,* one for words ending in *-er,* and one for words ending in *-or.* Then write each word from the list below in the correct column. Add at least five other words that have the same accent and spelling pattern to each column.

singer	director	soldier	governor
error	professor	scholar	pillar
founder	equator	commander	sugar

-ar	*-er*	*-or*
____________	____________	____________
____________	____________	____________
____________	____________	____________
____________	____________	____________
____________	____________	____________
____________	____________	____________
____________	____________	____________
____________	____________	____________
____________	____________	____________

At Home: Find other words that end in *-ar, -er,* or *-or.* Add these words to the three columns.

Name ______________________________

On the lines provided, write an antonym for each word below.

1. satisfactory ______________
2. enlightened ______________
3. staggered ______________
4. gushed ______________
5. stark ______________
6. brimming ______________

Write the definition of each boldface word below.

1. In the early Middle Ages, it was a **prevailing** belief that the world was flat.

____

2. Each player on the winning team walked off the field with a confident **swagger**.

____

3. She showed a lot of **spunk** and was not afraid to ask questions during the debate.

____

4. The defendant's **attorney** argued against the charges.

____

5. On the clear summer night, we saw a **meteor** briefly light up the sky.

____

6. He **rotated** in the swivel chair to reach the other papers on his desk.

____

7. Is that vision of the future **inevitable**, or can we change the outcome?

____

8. The old man's hands were as **gnarled** as a knotted tree.

____

Name ______________________________

Complete each group of words with the most appropriate choice from the words in the box. Not every word in the box will be used.

tyrant	legislature	landscape	tokens	representative
colonel	governor	progress	robot	suffrage

1. scenery
geography

____

2. judiciary
executive

____

3. counters
game board

____

4. monarch
dictator

____

Write a sentence for each of the words in parentheses, using context clues to show the meaning of the word. Underline the context clues.

1. (postpone) ______________________________

____

2. (humanity) ______________________________

____

____

3. (dangling) ______________________________

____

4. (swagger) ______________________________

____

Name ____________________

Read the following questions and think about the meaning of the boldfaced vocabulary words. Then answer each question with a complete sentence.

1. What is the temperature of water that a person can **scald** for cooking?
____

2. What are two activities that you can do without first getting **permission** from a family member or teacher? _______________
____

3. How might someone get to a library without bus **fare**? _______________
____

4. Whose **autograph** would you like to have, and why? _______________
____
____

5. What would you do if you **blurted** out a secret that you had promised to keep? _______________
____

6. Why couldn't you eat if your teeth were **clenched**? _______________
____
____

7. What tools might have **chiseled** a name in a block of stone?
____
____

8. What would be your idea of a way to spend a **spectacular** afternoon?
____
____

Name ______________________________

Read the story below, and then fill in the story structure chart.

All Kinds of Heroes
by Calliope Booth

Ana and Duane worked in the same office. Duane had a sports poster on his wall that showed a football hero. Ana just pointed to a small photograph on her desk, saying, "That's my hero."

Duane always wondered who the woman in the photograph was. Once he asked Ana, and she just smiled. "You ought to know," she said. Duane thought the woman looked familiar, but then he figured that it was just Ana's mother. He had seen her once, although he could not remember what she looked like.

Then one Friday he mentioned that his hero was coming into town for a sports event. Ana just pointed to the picture on her desk and said, "There are all kinds of heroes."

"Who is that woman?" asked Duane. "Is that your mother?"

"No," said Ana. "It's Rosa Parks. Her refusal to give up her bus seat in the 1950s started a civil rights protest that changed my life forever. So she's my hero. Remember, not every hero wears a sports uniform."

Characters: ______________________________

Setting: ______________________________

Problem or Conflict: ______________________________

____

Resolution: ______________________________

____

At Home: Make a story map for another short story. Use it to summarize the story orally for a family member or helper.

Name ___________________________________

As you read *Goin' Someplace Special,* fill in the Character and Setting Chart.

Character	Setting

How does the information you wrote in the Character and Setting Chart help you analyze the story structure of *Goin' Someplace Special*?

At Home: Have the student use the chart to retell the story.

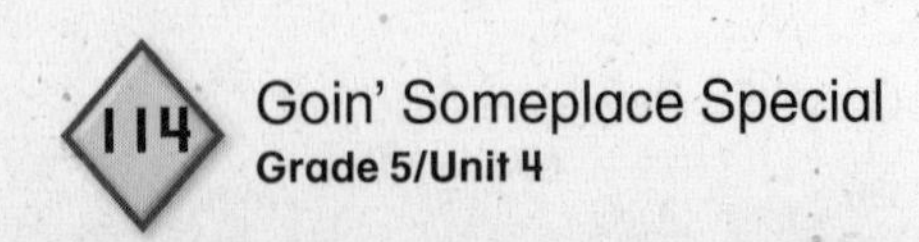

Name ____

As I read, I will pay attention to punctuation.

	This afternoon was a special occasion for Alexandra
8	and all the other students at the Metropolitan Music School.
18	Their annual spring recital was a chance to show off the hard
30	work and practice that they had put in during the winter.
41	Alexandra's chestnut brown hair was in a neat bun like a
52	ballerina's, tied with a velvet ribbon—not her usual bouncy
62	ponytail. Her long, blue velvet skirt fell gracefully to the floor
73	around the piano bench. She reached the end of the piece and
85	sat back. The people in the audience broke into applause.
95	"So talented for a teenager," one woman whispered to
104	her neighbor. "Isn't it a shame about.... " But her neighbor
114	couldn't hear the rest of the sentence because the applause
124	drowned it out.
127	Still sitting on the bench, the young pianist turned toward
137	the audience. "My next piece is one of my favorites, a short,
149	two-part invention by J. S. Bach," Alexandra said.
158	Again, she played beautifully, and the applause was loud
167	and enthusiastic. Waiting offstage in the wings, Alexandra's
175	parents smiled proudly. 178

Comprehension Check

1. How is Alexandra's appearance at her recital different from her usual appearance? **Compare and Contrast**

2. Why were Alexandra's parents proud of her? **Draw Conclusions**

	Words Read	–	Number of Errors	=	Words Correct Score
First Read		–		=	
Second Read		–		=	

At Home: Help the student read the passage, paying attention to the goal at the top of the page.

Name ______________________________

A **time line** is a series of events plotted along a chart. The events are placed in the order in which they happened.

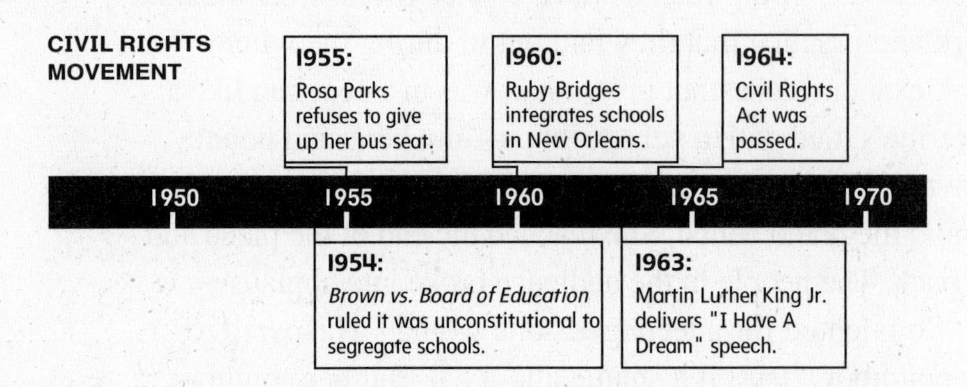

A. What are the advantages and disadvantages of presenting information in a time line instead of in an article? Write your answer in the chart.

Advantages of Time Line	Disadvantages of Time line

B. Write a brief paragraph about the time line above. Include at least three dates.

____

____

____

____

____

____

At Home: With a family member or helper, make a time line based on your life.

Name ____________________

Homophones are words that sound alike but are spelled differently and have different meanings. For example, *hear* means "to listen," and *here* means "in this place." When you write, be aware of homophones and make sure that you use the right one.

Look at each pair of homophones. Then write one sentence using each. If you wish you may write one sentence that contains both homophones. Be sure to use each word correctly.

1. fare fair

____

____

2. tows toes

____

____

3. ceiling sealing

____

____

4. aisle isle

____

____

5. hare hair

____

____

6. affect effect

____

____

____

At Home: Explain homophones to a family member or helper. Then work together to list more homophones. Use them to create a word search.

Name ______________________________

The **/əl/ sound** and **/ən/ sound** that you hear in words can be spelled in many different ways. The /əl/ can be spelled ***al, el, il,*** or ***le***. The /ən/ can be spelled ***en, in, an, on,*** or ***ain.***

Underline the letters that spell the final /əl/ or /ən/ sound in each word. Then write a word from the box that spells the same sound in the same way.

able	button	certain	barrel	little
pelican	raisin	global	vowel	widen
wooden	fiddle	tighten	thimble	turtle
royal	ribbon	dragon	general	frightened

1. angel ____________
2. bacon ____________
3. sharpen ____________
4. vessel ____________
5. captain ____________
6. basin ____________
7. broken ____________
8. terrible ____________
9. human ____________
10. signal ____________
11. reason ____________
12. happen ____________
13. ripple ____________
14. lesson ____________
15. capital ____________
16. nibble ____________
17. handle ____________
18. women ____________
19. festival ____________
20. sudden ____________

At Home: Search a newspaper for five additional words that end with the sound of /əl/ or /ən/. Underline the letters that spell the sound.

Write the clues for this crossword puzzle.

									1. a			
									r			
									r			
									o			
				2. n					y			
			3. b	e	h	4. a	v	i	o	r		
				s		r						6. s
5. s				t		o						e
t				l		u						c
7. u	n	p	l	e	a	s	a	n	t			l
n				d		i						u
n						n						d
e						8. g	l	i	m	p	s	e
d												d

Across:

3. ____________________

7. ____________________

8. ____________________

Down

1. ____________________

2. ____________________

4. ____________________

5. ____________________

6. ____________________

Name ______________________________

Read each passage below. On the line provided, write whether the author's main purpose is to persuade, to inform, or to entertain. Then write an additional sentence that is consistent with the author's purpose.

1. Author's purpose: ______________

If you cross paths with a wild animal, you should leave it alone. Frightening any wild animal stresses it and puts it in danger. Also some animals may attack you if they see you as threatening. You should observe wild animals from a safe distance.

____

____

____

2. Author's purpose: ______________

Skunks are small mammals that weigh only about eight or nine pounds. They move slowly but may cover several miles while looking for food. They eat almost anything, including rodents, lizards, garbage, and even poisonous insects.

____

____

____

3. Author's purpose: ______________

Sara and her sister were playing basketball in their backyard. The ball rolled into the bushes. Sara ran to get the ball, but before she could reach down and grab it, a furry shape suddenly walked right in front of it. "Ah! It's a skunk!" Sara shouted with fear.

____

____

____

At Home: With a family member or helper, look at a newspaper or magazine. Find one article or story that persuades, one that informs, and one that entertains.

Name ______________________________

As you read *Carlos and the Skunk*, fill in the Author's Purpose Chart.

Clues	Author's Purpose

How does the information you wrote in the Author's Purpose Chart help you evaluate *Carlos and the Skunk*?

At Home: Have the student use the chart to retell the story.

Name ____________________

As I read, I will pay attention to intonation.

	Like most animals, insects prefer to avoid danger. Many
9	predators, such as birds and skunks, hunt insects for food. Insects
20	will run or fly to get away from them. Such good avoidance
32	behaviors keep these insects alive. But running away is not the
43	only way insects avoid danger.
48	Insects have excellent eyesight, which helps to keep them safe
58	from predators. Special sense organs on their antennae and feet
68	also alert them to danger. They can "hear" sound vibrations in
79	the air as well as feel them through the ground or on other
92	surfaces where they live.
96	Some insects use disguises to stay out of danger. Green
106	lacewing larvae are both predators and prey. As predators, these
116	young lacewings hunt insects that have soft bodies, such as
126	aphids. As prey they need to hide from predators who want to
138	snatch them up for a meal. So green lacewing larvae cover
149	themselves with debris. For example, they might take the bodies
159	of aphids they have eaten and stick them on their backs. 170

Comprehension Check

1. What is the main idea of this passage? **Main Idea and Details**

2. How do insects use their antennae and feet to protect them from danger? **Main Idea and Details**

	Words Read	–	Number of Errors	=	Words Correct Score
First Read		–		=	
Second Read		–		=	

At Home: Help the student read the passage, paying attention to the goal at the top of the page.

Name ____________________

A magazine article has many features that are designed to catch your attention and help you find information. For example, the title and **headings** give you a quick look at what the article will be about. The byline tells who wrote the article. The **deck** is a short preview of the article.

Write a magazine article about animal self-defense. Include a deck and headings.

At Home: Find a magazine article without a deck and write one for it.

Name ______________________________

Practice

Vocabulary Strategy: Context Clues

Write the definition of each boldfaced word on the line provided. Underline the context clues that help you figure out the definition.

1. Walking on the sand was difficult, but we **trudged** along as best we could.

____

2. The **rickety** bridge swayed and creaked even in the gentlest breeze.

____

3. With a striking white stripe against its black fur, a skunk certainly looks **conspicuous**.

____

4. Skunks look for food mainly at night and usually start **foraging** at sunset.

____

5. The rabbit was so startled that it ran into a tree and was momentarily stunned from the **collision**.

____

6. The deer's **initial** reaction to danger was to stay still, but then it raced away.

____

7. I read a full-length article on those insects in a book, but an **abridged** version is online.

____

8. Some animals **cope** with danger by hiding, but other animals respond to danger by facing their enemies.

____

9. He was writing the **manuscript** so it could be printed by the newspaper.

____

10. The **menacing** dog frightens the young girls with its loud bark.

____

At Home: Write new sentences for five of the words above. Ask a family member or helper to underline the context clues in your sentences.

Name ____________________

Accented syllables may have vowel sounds that can be spelled in different ways. For example, the words ***rowdy*** and ***rousing*** have the same vowel sound in the accented syllable, but the syllable is spelled two different ways.

A. Read the words below. Listen to the vowel sound in each accented syllable. Then look at the headings of the chart, and sort each word from the list into the correct column.

arousing	coward	toiling	boundary	loyal
caution	joyful	flawless	fountain	laundry
drawing	powder	shower	calling	thoughtful

/ou/ sound in *allow*	/oi/ sound in *coiling*	/ô/ sound in *applause*

B. Use your completed chart to write the different ways to spell each vowel sound.

1. spellings with /ou/ sound in **allow** ____________
2. spellings with /oi/ sound in **coiling** ____________
3. spellings with /ô/ sound in **applause** ____________

At Home: Find a new word for each of the different spellings of the vowel sounds above. Ask a family member or helper to check your work.

Name ______________________

A. Write the word from the box that belongs in each group.

compelled	presidential	disrespectful
unenthusiastically	succeed	preoccupied

1. senatorial, mayoral, ______________
2. follow, come next, ______________
3. urged, forced, ______________
4. unexcitedly, unwillingly, ______________
5. rude, insulting, ______________
6. concerned, absorbed, ______________

B. Write four sentences, using a word from the box in each one.

1. ______________________________________

2. ______________________________________

3. ______________________________________

4. ______________________________________

Name ____

A. Provide an example from your own knowledge about the generalizations below.

1. It is important to encourage people to vote.

____

____

____

2. Most people who do not vote do not have a very important reason.

____

____

____

B. Now make two of your own generalizations about voting. Make sure that your generalizations are based both on facts and on your own knowledge.

____

____

____

____

____

____

____

____

____

____

____

____

____

At Home: Look for generalizations in an advertisement. Find facts in a book or on the Internet that support the advertisement's claims.

Name ________________________________

As you read "Getting Out the Vote", fill in the Generalizations Chart.

Information from Text	
Prior Knowledge	
Generalizations	

How does the information you wrote in this Generalizations Chart help you evaluate "Getting Out the Vote"?

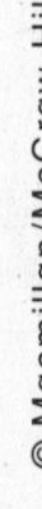

At Home: Have the student use the chart to retell the story.

As I read, I will pay attention to pauses.

	On May 29 the Virginians presented a whole new plan for a national
12	government to the other delegates. Delegates soon called it the
22	Virginia Plan.
24	Their plan was complex. They believed the country needed a stronger
35	national government. Yet they also knew that strong governments could
45	misuse their powers. The challenge was to create a government that had
57	the strength to meet the needs of the nation, but one that had limits
71	as well.
73	At the heart of their plan was a Congress made up of two houses.
87	One house would be made up of elected representatives. Members of
98	the other house, called the Senate, would not be elected. They would
110	simply be chosen by state governments. This Congress would write the
121	nation's laws. Both houses had to pass a law for it to take effect.
135	The Virginia Plan also called for a national president. The presidency
146	was a new idea. The states had no president under the Articles of
159	Confederation. Under the new plan, the **presidential** powers would
168	differ from those of Congress. Congress alone would write and pass
179	laws. The president's main duty would be to carry out the laws. 191

Comprehension Check

1. What challenge did the Virginians face when they came up with their plan for government? **Main Idea and Details**

2. Under the Virginia Plan, what was the role of Congress? **Main Idea and Details**

	Words Read	–	Number of Errors	=	Words Correct Score
First Read		–		=	
Second Read		–		=	

At Home: Help the student read the passage, paying attention to the goal at the top of the page.

Name ______________________________

Suppose that you have a book on American history that you are using to find information for a research paper. Use the table to help you identify the book part that you would use to find the information below.

Parts	Information
Title Page	book title, author name, publisher, publication date
Table of Contents	a list of major book features, such as chapters, illustrations, glossaries, and indexes, with the starting page number of each feature
Chapter Titles and Headings	names of each chapter and major chapter divisions
Index	an alphabetical list of the book's topics and the page numbers that apply to each item
Glossary	an alphabetical list of important word definitions
Endnotes	additional information about chapter contents
Bibliography	a list of research sources that the author used

1. the page number on which Chapter 2 begins ______________
2. the meaning of *poll tax* ______________
3. additional notes about a presidential election ______________
4. titles of other books about American history ______________
5. the author's middle name ______________
6. the names of the major sections in Chapter 4 ______________
____
7. If a book did not have an index, what could you do to find the information you want? ______________
8. Where can you find the chapter titles? ______________

At Home: List the parts of one of your textbooks, including any not mentioned in the table above.

Name ______________________________

Write the meaning of the boldfaced word in each phrase. Use the table.

Prefix	Meanings	Suffix	Meaning
dis-	not, opposite of	*-al*	of, having to do with
inter-	between	*-ance*	state or quality of
mis-	*wrong*	*-ful*	full of
re-	again	*-ist*	one of
un-	not, opposite of	*-ment*	state or quality of

1. newspaper **cartoonist** ______________________________

2. **disrespectful** behavior ______________________________

3. very **thoughtful** ______________________________

4. **reappearance** of an issue ______________________________

5. **misstatement** of facts ______________________________

6. **unconstitutional** law ______________________________

7. **residential** community ______________________________

8. **international** trip ______________________________

At Home: Look through a newspaper or magazine for five words that have prefixes and suffixes. Then use each word in a sentence.

Name ______________________________

Homographs are words that are spelled alike but have different meanings. Sometimes words that are homographs will be accented, or stressed, on different syllables. The part of speech and the meaning of the word depend on which syllable is accented.

Find the homograph in each sentence and circle the accented syllable. Then write the definition.

1. Many voters refuse to vote for members of another party.

   ____

   Street cleaners picked up refuse after the election.

   ____

2. Contrary to popular belief, rain does fall in the desert.

   ____

   The senator would not desert her party's principles.

   ____

3. The mayor signed a contract to buy new voting equipment.

   ____

   Your pupils will contract when in bright light.

   ____

4. There is only a minute chance of snow on Election Day.

   ____

   It takes only a minute or two to cast your vote.

   ____

5. Do people need permits to put up signs for candidates?

   ____

   The city permits residents to put signs on their own property.

   ____

At Home: With a family member or helper, write two riddles about homographs or about using homographs.

Name ______________________________

Answer each question in a complete sentence. Use the vocabulary word in your response.

1. Why do you think that **damages** from some storms cost so much?
____
____

2. What kinds of **property** might people own? ______________________________
____
____

3. What are some ways that the government could make facts **available** to many people? ______________________________
____

4. What happens to air when it makes **contact** with something very hot or cold?
____
____

5. Where can you see Earth's **atmosphere** clearly? ______________________________
____
____

6. Why do some storms cause more **destruction** than others? ______________________________
____
____

7. How would you describe **hurricanes**? ______________________________
____

8. What makes an ocean **surge** so dangerous to people living near water?
____
____

Name ______________________________

Below write five descriptions about hurricanes. Use descriptive words such as *first, next, then, when,* and *finally*. A description has been done for you.

1. First, condensation takes place. Then the clouds thicken. When fully formed, a hurricane has an eye at its center.

2. ______________________________

3. ______________________________

4. ______________________________

5. ______________________________

At Home: Look for descriptions of one kind of storm that can occur in your area.

Name ______________________________

As you read *Hurricanes,* fill in the Description Chart.

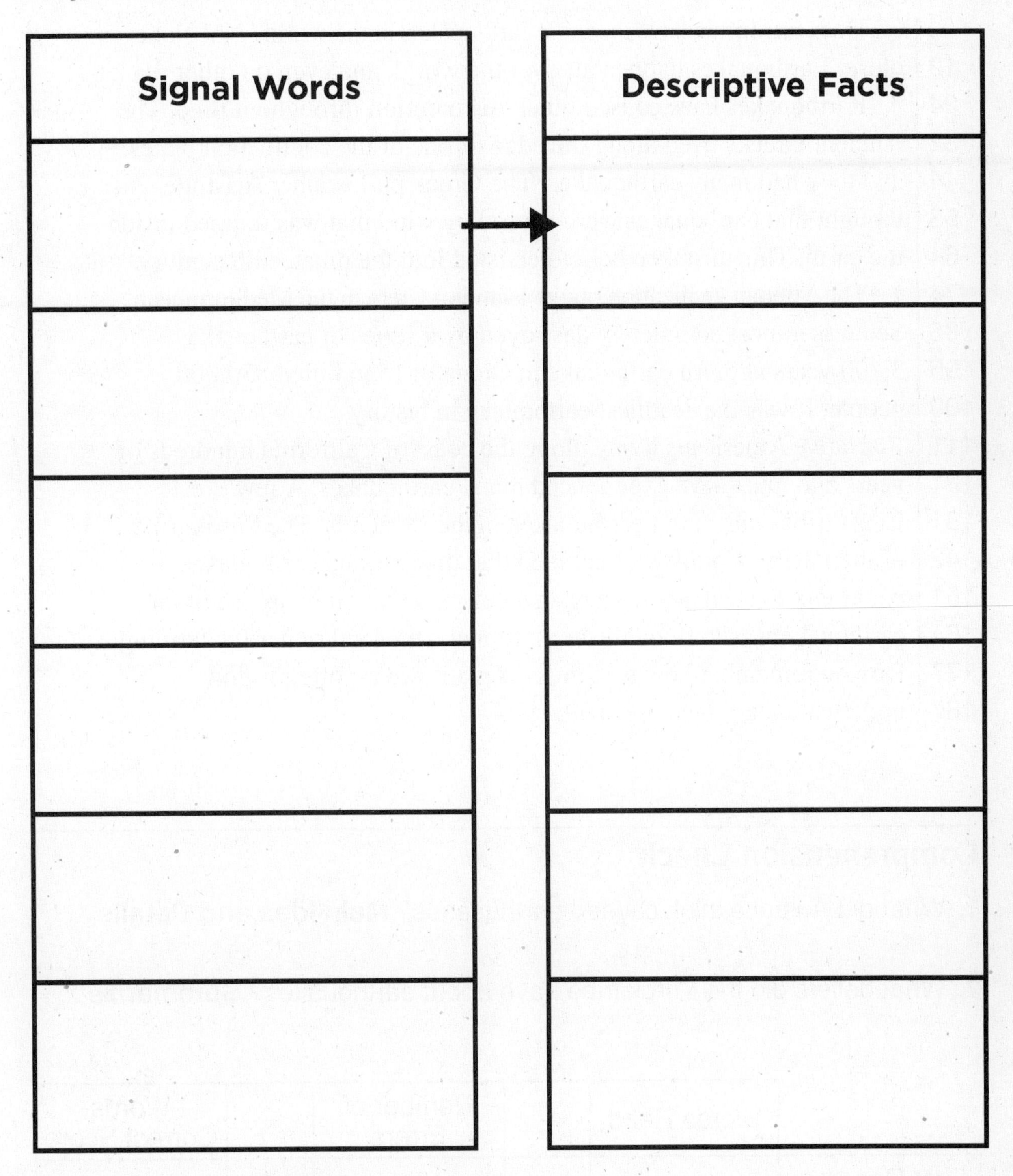

How does the information you wrote in the Description Chart help you analyze the text structure of *Hurricanes*?

At Home: Have the student use the chart to retell the story.

Name ______________________________

As I read, I will pay attention to pronunciation.

| | Does California have the most earthquakes in the world? No! Not even
12 | close. Earthquakes happen all over the world, and even on other planets.
24 | Earthquakes have caused much **destruction** throughout time. The
32 | Ancient Greeks lived along the edge of one of the continental plates,
44 | and they had many earthquakes. The Greek philosopher Aristotle
53 | thought that earthquakes were caused by wind that was trapped inside
64 | the earth. This mistaken belief persisted into the nineteenth century.
74 | The Minoan civilization on the island of Crete in the Mediterranean
85 | Sea was almost completely destroyed by a series of earthquakes
95 | 3,700 years ago. An earthquake in China in 1556 killed 830,000
103 | people. It was the deadliest earthquake in history.
111 | Native Americans living along the coast of California hundreds of
121 | years ago must have experienced many earthquakes. A few West
131 | Coast tribes talk about earthquakes in their legends. The Yurok tribe
142 | of the Pacific Northwest imagined that thunder and earthquakes
151 | could talk to each other. They also believed that one purpose of an
164 | earthquake was to flood the coast to make the land richer for farming.
177 | Do you remember how tsunamis, or giant waves, often follow
187 | underwater earthquakes? 189

Comprehension Check

1. What did Aristotle think caused earthquakes? **Main Idea and Details**

2. What beliefs did the Yurok tribe have about earthquakes? **Summarize**

	Words Read	–	Number of Errors	=	Words Correct Score
First Read		–		=	
Second Read		–		=	

At Home: Help the student read the passage, paying attention to the goal at the top of the page.

Name ____________________

Poets use a variety of techniques in their poems, including **personification,** which is giving human characteristics to an animal, a thing, or an idea, **imagery,** which is the use of description to create vivid pictures in a reader's mind, and **onomatopoeia,** which is using a word to imitate the sound of an action or object.

Read each example of poetry, and decide what technique the poet used. Underline the words that tell you. Then write a new line on a similar topic, using the same technique.

1. Acorns clatter onto the concrete below. ____________________

____

____

2. The river rose from its bed and wandered about the neighborhood.

____

____

3. Shiny pink petals spread across grey stone. ____________________

____

____

4. Night winds lick the grass but do not consume it. ____________________

____

____

5. Flocks of golden finches glitter on black branches. ____________________

____

____

At Home: Look at several poems about nature to find examples of personification, imagery, and onomatopoeia.

Name ______________________________

Practice

Vocabulary Strategy: Multiple-Meaning Words

Write two different meanings for each word. Use a dictionary if you need help.

1. advance ______________________________
____

2. atmosphere ______________________________
____

3. bands ______________________________
____

4. form ______________________________
____

5. peak ______________________________
____

6. pressure ______________________________
____

7. spinning ______________________________
____

8. tone ______________________________
____

At Home: With a family member or helper, search for multiple-meaning words in books and magazines. See who can find the most words in five minutes.

Name ______________________________

butcher	creature	enclosure	composure
future	gesture	exposure	legislature
mixture	measure	nature	pleasure
rancher	leisure	treasure	azure

A. Read the headings of the chart. Then write each word from the list in the correct column.

***/chər/* sound**	

***/zhər/* sound**	

B. Complete each sentence to explain ways to spell each sound.

1. The ending sound in **culture** ______________________________

____

____

2. The ending sound in **measure** ______________________________

____

____

At Home: Find words in a newspaper or magazine that end with one of the sounds that you studied today.

Name ______________________________

Read each sentence beginning. Think about the meaning of the underlined vocabulary word. Then complete each sentence to show the meaning of that word.

1. When the baker came to the riverbank, he ______________________________

____

2. The most colorful wares at the market ______________________________

____

3. The company hired a treasurer to ______________________________

____

4. The store's merchandise was ______________________________

____

5. One way to educate someone is ______________________________

____

6. Everyone had burdens that ______________________________

____

7. One way to show appreciation is ______________________________

____

8. An example of an unfortunate day might be ______________________________

____

Name ______________________________

Write a paragraph about trickster tales for each purpose below.

Purpose: To Entertain ______________________________

Purpose: To Inform ______________________________

Purpose: To Persuade ______________________________

At Home: Look for three pieces of writing in which the author's purpose is clearly to entertain, to inform, or to persuade. Write the clues that helped you.

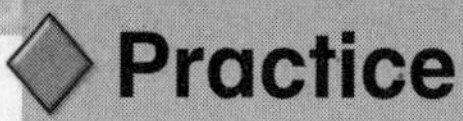

Comprehension: Author's Purpose

Name ______________________________

As you read *The Catch of the Day,* fill in the Author's Purpose Chart.

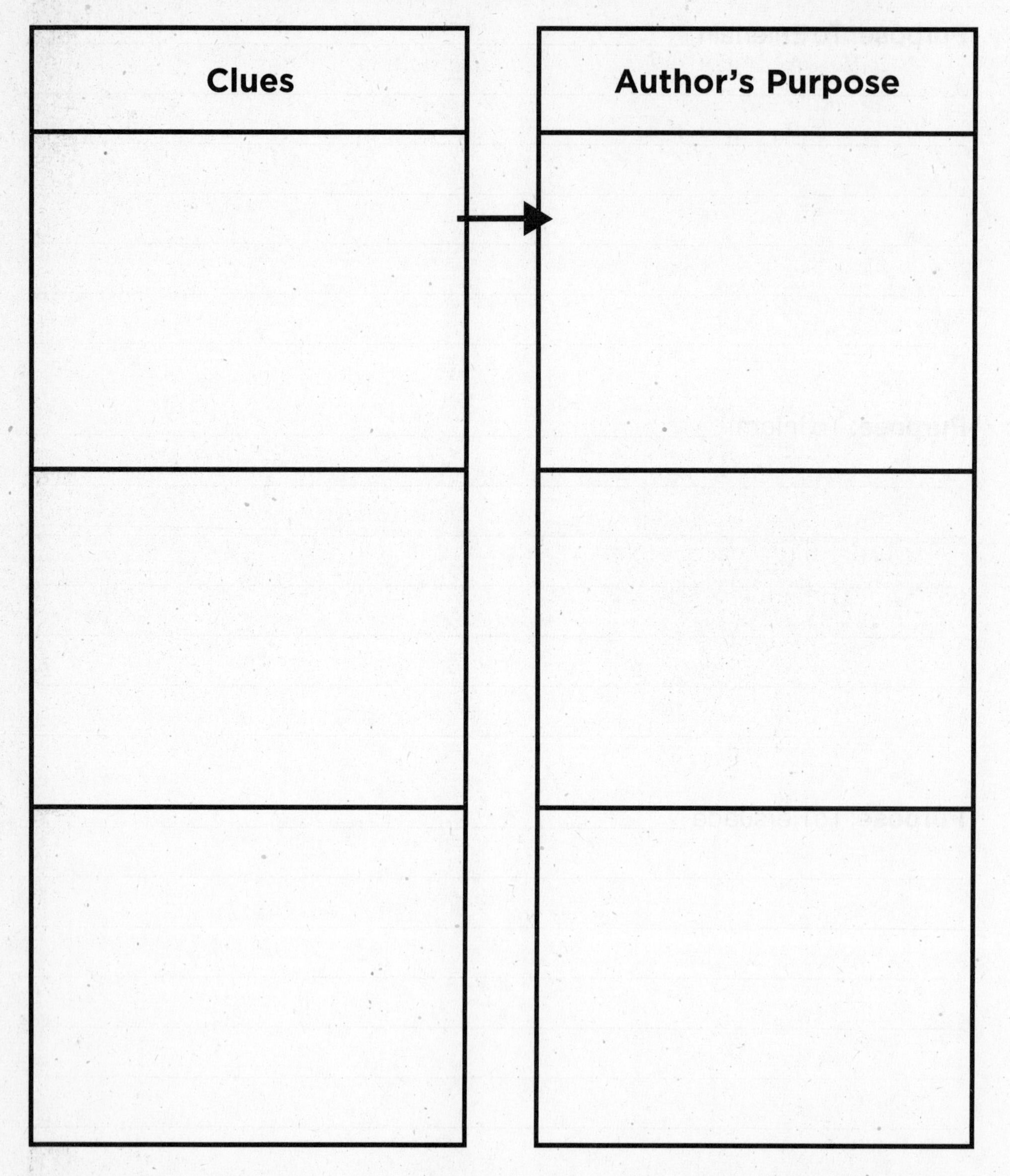

How does the information you wrote in the Author's Purpose Chart help you evaluate *The Catch of the Day*?

At Home: Have the student use the chart to retell the story.

Name ______________________________

As I read, I will pay attention to tempo.

	Thor enters, dragging Loki along with him. Thor is
9	*holding Sif's hair in his other hand. He stops center stage*
20	*and shakes the hair in Loki's face.*
27	**Thor:** Look what you've done, Loki, you wicked
35	trickster! How dare you cut off my wife's beautiful hair?
45	**Loki:** I'm sorry, I'm so sorry, Thor. I . . . I just thought it
57	would be funny for Sif to wake up and find her hair gone.
70	Really, the scissors almost seemed to take over my hand and
81	make me do it!
85	**Thor:** I don't want to hear any excuses! Sif is crying her
97	eyes out, and you think it's funny! Do you know how long it
110	took for her hair to grow that long?
118	**Loki:** I'll get the hair back for Sif, I promise I will. I'll
131	find her some hair that's even more beautiful. In fact . . . in
142	fact, I'll find her hair that's spun out of real gold.
153	**Thor:** You're going to find hair spun out of real gold? Is
165	this another one of your tricks, Loki?
172	**Loki:** No, Thor, I mean it. I promise you, I'll do it. 184

Comprehension Check

1. What does Loki blame for his trick? **Main Idea and Details**

2. How does Loki plan to solve his problem? **Plot**

	Words Read	–	Number of Errors	=	Words Correct Score
First Read		–		=	
Second Read		–		=	

At Home: Help the student read the passage, paying attention to the goal at the top of the page.

Name ______________________________

Read the fable and answer the questions below.

A fox fell into a deep well. A goat walked by and stopped to ask what the fox was doing in the abyss. The fox replied, "A great drought will soon strike, and I am down here drinking my fill. This well is almost a desert. You better come down, too, so you don't die of thirst."

Without thinking, the goat jumped into the well. The fox quickly scampered up the goat's back and horns and climbed out. Then he looked down at the goat and said, "The next time someone tells you to do something, look before you leap!"

1. What human qualities do the characters have? ______________________________
____

2. What problem did the fox have? ______________________________
____

3. What character weakness does the goat have? ______________________________
____

4. How does the fox trick the goat? ______________________________
____

5. What moral does the fable teach? ______________________________
____

6. What metaphors can you find in the fable? What do they compare? ______
____
____
____
____

At Home: Write a short fable and read it aloud. Include a moral and a metaphor.

Name ______________________________

Analogies show **relationships** between pairs of words. Word pairs can be related in different ways. Some word pairs show a relationship between a worker and the worker's activity, product, tools, or place of work.

A. Write a word to complete each of the following analogies.

1. Nibble is to eat as sip is to ______________.
2. Baker is to ______________ as weaver is to cloth.
3. ______________ is to book as artist is to painting.
4. Doctor is to healing as ______________ is to flying.
5. Chef is to cook as carpenter is to ______________.
6. Driver is to ______________ as conductor is to train.
7. Teacher is to school as ______________ is to hospital.
8. ______________ is to apples as vine is to grapes.
9. ______________ is to poet as song is to singer.
10. Governor is to state as president is to ______________.

B. Write five analogies of your own.

11. ______________________________
12. ______________________________
13. ______________________________
14. ______________________________
15. ______________________________

At Home: Write five more analogies. Make all five part of the same category. For example, all five analogies could be about animals.

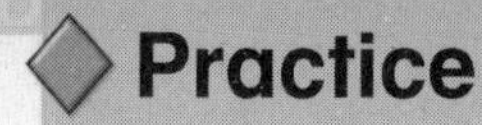

Name ___________________________________

The suffixes ***-ance*** and ***-ence*** mean "the state or quality of." They are suffixes with unstressed vowels and can change verbs to nouns or adjectives to nouns.

assistance	attendance	dependence	ignorance
importance	persistence	radiance	residence
substance	distance	hesitance	inference

Read the headings of the chart. Say the words aloud and listen for the stressed syllable.

First syllable is stressed	Second syllable is stressed

Which words in the chart can be changed to an adjective? ______________

____

____

____

____

At Home: Find five words in a newspaper or a magazine that end with *-ence* or *-ance*. Sort them in a chart.

Name ______________________________

A. For each pair of words below, write a single sentence that uses both words.

1. hurricanes, spectacular: ______________________________
____
2. autograph, available: ______________________________
____
3. behavior, arousing: ______________________________
____
4. compelled, presidential: ______________________________
____
5. treasurer, property: ______________________________
____

B. On the lines provided, write the word that has a similar meaning to the given word, but has either a stronger or weaker connotation. Choose from the words in the box. Some words will not be used.

available	stunned	unpleasant	atmosphere	destruction
disrespectful	surge	burdens	appreciation	unfortunate

6. shocked ________________
7. damage ________________
8. duties ________________
9. terrible ________________
10. rude ________________

Name ______________________________

A. Write a definition for each boldface word below.

1. Her lips were **clenched** as she tried to keep silent.

____

2. Tom did poorly on the test because he was **preoccupied**.

____

3. A **surge** in electricity can damage delicate appliances such as computers.

____

4. The blacksmith sold his **wares** at the village market.

____

5. The sailor **blurted** out the treasure's secret location.

____

B. Choose five words from the box, and write a sentence for each.

scald	glimpse	nestled	secluded
contact	damages	merchandise	unenthusiastically

6. ____

____

7. ____

____

8. ____

____

9. ____

____

10. ____

____

Name ________________________________

Read each sentence beginning. Think about the meaning of the underlined vocabulary word. Then complete each sentence to show the meaning of the word.

1. In order to <u>triumph</u> in tonight's game, the hockey team ____________________
____.

2. In very cold places, people perform <u>labor</u> to ____________________
____.

3. People may <u>abandon</u> a voyage to the South Pole ____________________
____.

4. One reason that the South Pole is mainly <u>uninhabited</u> is because
____.

5. The crew <u>dismantled</u> the ship ____________________
____.

6. In <u>frigid</u> places, people ____________________
____.

7. If conditions are <u>treacherous</u>, then they are ____________________
____.

8. An <u>expedition</u> to the South Pole might also be called ____________________
____.

Name ______________________________

Read the definitions below, then complete the chart by listing an action and a result for each problem.

Problem – something to be worked out or solved

Action – what was done to fix or solve the problem

Result – what happens as a result of the action; the effect or outcome

Problem	Action	Result
The *Endurance* begins breaking up.		
The men must get off the ice because the ice floe will eventually be carried out to sea.		
A ship might never come to Elephant Island to rescue the crew.		
Shackleton reaches the whaling station, but the men on Elephant Island still must be rescued.		

At Home: Retell the story of Shackleton and the *Endurance* to a family member or helper. Think of three or more words that describe Shackleton and his crew as problem solvers.

Name ____________________

As you read *Spirit of Endurance,* fill in the Problem and Solution Map.

Problem

Attempt → **Outcome**

Attempt → **Outcome**

Attempt → **Outcome**

Solution

How does the information you wrote in the Problem and Solution Map help you generate questions about *Spirit of Endurance*?

At Home: Have the student use the chart to retell the story.

Name ____

As I read, I will pay attention to pronunciation.

	Professor Babcock will tell you that 160 million years ago, Antarctica
10	was very different than it is today. It was warmer. When he looks at
24	the frozen land in Antartica, Professor Babcock can imagine what was
35	there three millions of years ago. He says, "I see ponds, forests and some
49	reptiles swimming around."
52	The fossils that Professor Babcock found are proof that Antarctica
62	once had a warmer climate. Fossils are arthropods. Arthropods are
72	animals like spiders, crustaceans, and insects. Most arthropods don't
81	have body parts, like teeth or toes, that easily turn into fossils.
93	Antarctica is one of the only places in the world where fossils of
106	arthropods can be found. One question Professor Babcock is trying to
117	answer is why these animals did turn to fossils in Antarctica. According
129	to Professor Babcock, two things have to happen in order for a fossil
142	to form. First, no predator can eat the creature. Second, something has to
155	happen to turn it into rock.
161	The fossils were found in the Trans-Antarctic Mountains. Long ago,
171	these mountains were active volcanoes. Professor Babcock thinks that
180	these little arthropods lived in pools that were hot because they were
192	close to volcanic vents. That cut down on the number of predators. 204

Comprehension Check

1. How can Professor Babcock prove that Antarctica was once warmer? **Summarize**

2. Why is it difficult to find fossils of arthropods? **Main Idea and Details**

	Words Read	–	Number of Errors	=	Words Correct Score
First Read		–		=	
Second Read		–		=	

At Home: Help the student read the passage, paying attention to the goal at the top of the page.

Name ______________________________

A primary source is an illustration, a **letter**, a **journal**, or other information created by someone who witnessed actual events.

A. Write a journal entry about what it is like to live at the North Pole. Describe what you do each day.

____
____
____
____
____
____
____
____
____

B. Write a letter to a friend back home about your new school at the North Pole. Describe what your classroom, teacher, and classmates are like.

____
____
____
____
____
____
____
____

At Home: Identify information from old letters or photographs about places, fashions, or technology from another time period.

Name ______________________________

An affix is a word part such as a prefix or suffix that can be added to a base or root word. For the items below, use affixes, base words, or root words to make new words. Note changes in spelling. Then use each new word in a sentence that correctly shows the meaning of the word.

Base Word + Affixes	Root Word + Affixes
un- + do = undo un- + do + able = undoable	in- + spect = inspect in- spect + ion = inspection

1. mountain + -eer + -ing ____________________

____

____

2. un- + in- + habit + -ed ____________________

____

____

3. sur- + viv + -al ____________________

____

____

4. un- + forget + -able ____________________

____

____

5. pre- + dict + -ion ____________________

____

____

At Home: Look in newspapers or magazines to find five words that are made up of a base or root word with one or more affixes. Write a sentence for each word.

Name ______________________________

Some words that are spelled with the letter *g* have a hard *g* sound. *Bag, rug, gone,* and *igloo* are examples of words with the hard *g* sound.

Some words have a **soft g** sound. *Age, edge, engine, join,* and *enjoy* are examples of words with a soft g sound. Some words with the soft *g* sound are spelled with *j* instead of with *g.*

A. In each sentence, underline every *g* that has a soft *g* sound.

1. Getting the gear off the boat was an urgent problem.
2. The men put a great deal of energy into the task and did not argue.
3. The sight of the boat's breaking apart was tragic.
4. Could the crew imagine what they were up against?
5. Dragging their gear more than 300 miles was a giant task.
6. The gentlemen of the crew took on the challenge.
7. They began moving their baggage across the Antarctic region.
8. The story of their courage has become a legend.
9. They faced hunger and grave danger from the sea.
10. How would they get over the mountain range on South Georgia Island?

B. Write five sentences each with two soft *g* words.

11. ______________________________
12. ______________________________
13. ______________________________
14. ______________________________
15. ______________________________

At Home: With a family member or helper, write five more words in which the letter *g* sounds like *j*.

Name ______________________________

Read each clue below to complete the crossword puzzle.

Across

4. Wild confusion

5. Plan

6. Society; type of culture

8. Bounced back or off

Down

1. Customary; conventional

2. Complicated

3. Person who has been sent away; lonely wanderer

7. Lack of

Name ______________________________

The **theme** is the overall idea that the author wants to tell in a story. Sometimes a theme can be a lesson, such as "don't lie." Other times the theme is just a statement, such as "family members help one another."

For each story, read the theme and the passage. Then finish the story, keeping in mind the story's theme.

Theme: It's fine to be different.

Amy really enjoyed playing soccer. Her favorite part was stealing the ball from the defense and scoring goals. Amy was really good at soccer, but none of her friends played. Stacy, Juan, and Julie preferred to play basketball.

____

____

____

____

____

Theme: Don't judge people by their appearances.

I had to admit that I was disappointed that I was assigned Edmund as a lab partner. He seemed to be the only boy in my school who enjoyed being alone. I rarely saw him eat with or speak to anyone at recess. And when I would see him with someone, he always wore a scowl on his face and didn't say much.

____

____

____

____

____

At Home: Discuss a movie or a show that you watched. Identify the theme and write a short paragraph about it.

Name ______________________________

As you read *Weslandia*, fill in the Theme Chart.

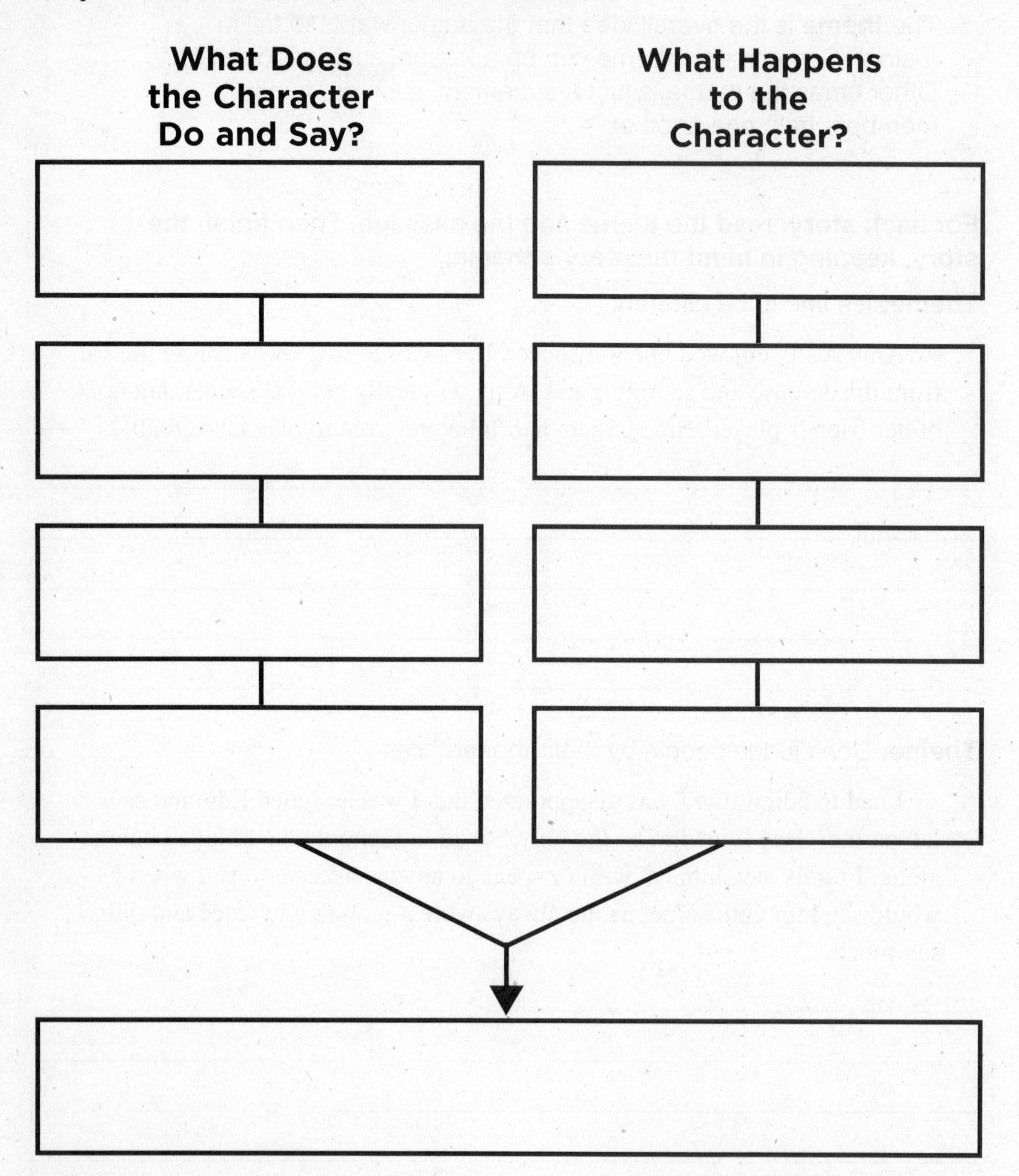

How does the information you wrote in the Theme Chart help you make inferences and analyze *Weslandia*?

At Home: Have the student use the chart to retell the story.

Name ______________________________

As I read, I will pay attention to punctuation.

Morgan and Megan are 10-year-old twin sisters. They look alike, they
11 sound alike, and often they even dress alike. But there's one thing that
24 Morgan and Megan do not do alike and that's gardening. Both girls belong
37 to the town gardening club and have for several years. But while Morgan can
51 grow just about anything and everything, Megan can hardly ever get
62 anything to sprout.
65 "I'm considering quitting the gardening club," Megan said one day to her
77 sister.
78 "Mom won't like that one bit," said Morgan as she pruned old blooms
91 from her prize-winning rose bush.
96 You see, Morgan and Megan come from a long line of champion
108 gardeners. Millie Milton, Morgan and Megan's mom, raised them to be
119 gardeners from birth. They have been digging in dirt since before they could
132 walk.
133 "I know," said Megan. "She will really treat me like an **outcast**. But I
147 already feel like one since I'm so terrible at gardening." Megan looked over
160 at her rose bush, which was wilted and bare.
169 "Maybe you should stick it out a little longer," said Morgan. "You never
182 know what can happen." 186

Comprehension Check

1. Compare and contrast Morgan and Megan? **Compare And Contrast**

2. Why does Megan want to quit gardening? **Make Inferences**

	Words Read	–	Number of Errors	=	Words Correct Score
First Read		–		=	
Second Read		–		=	

At Home: Help the student read the passage, paying attention to the goal at the top of the page.

Name ________________________________

◆ **Practice**

Text Features: Hyperlinks and Keys Words

Read the article below, then answer the questions.

Recently scientists have developed a new kind of fruit called the *pluot*. This fruit is a combination of a plum and an apricot. When one plant is combined with another to develop a new plant, the new plant is called a hybrid. Other hybrids include square watermelons, blue potatoes, and purple cauliflower. Hybrid fruits often stay fresher during shipping, which is a real advantage for supermarkets and their customers. Don't be surprised to see more and more unusual fruits and vegetables, which may make the produce section of the supermarket look very different.

1. Which key words could have been used to reach this article if it was on a Web page? ________________________________

____

2. Which words would you make hyperlinks to go to a new page about other hybrid fruits or vegetables? ________________________________

____

3. How could you find more information about the two fruits a pluot is made from? ________________________________

____

____

4. What could you do to make sure the information in this article is accurate?

____

____

At Home: Find out which encyclopedias are available online in your town or city library.

Name ______________________________

Dictionaries contain more than just meanings, pronunciations, and spellings. They also provide **word origins** or histories for some words. Information about where a word comes from is usually found in brackets and might look like this:

daisy [from Old English *daeges,* meaning "of the day" and *eage*, meaning "eye"]

Look up each of the following words in your dictionary. List each word's origin.

1. squirrel ______________________________

____

2. tomato ______________________________

____

3. barbecue ______________________________

____

4. poinsettia ______________________________

____

5. alphabet ______________________________

____

6. currant ______________________________

____

At Home: Ask a family member or helper to help you use an online or print dictionary to find the origins of these words: *zero, sequoia, decibel,* and *python.*

Name ____________________

Use each word below in a complete sentence that shows the word's meaning. You may use a dictionary if you need help.

1. flour ____________________

2. flower ____________________

3. suite ____________________

4. sweet ____________________

5. presents ____________________

6. presence ____________________

7. peer ____________________

8. pier ____________________

9. current ____________________

10. currant ____________________

At Home: Look up these homophones and use each of them in a sentence: *council* and *counsel*.

Name ______________________

instill combined naturalist vacant diverse

A. Write the word from the list above that best completes each group.

1. empty, unoccupied, ______________
2. unified, joined, ______________
3. teach, instruct, ______________
4. biologist, environmentalist, ______________
5. different, varied, ______________

B. Use each vocabulary word in a sentence about learning from nature.

6. ____
____

7. ____
____

8. ____
____

9. ____
____

10. ____
____

Name ______________________________

Read the paragraph to find four cause-and-effect relationships.

In the early nineteenth century, President Thomas Jefferson was considering the purchase of a huge area of land from France, and he asked Merriwether Lewis to explore the new territory. This territory, which would later be known as the Louisiana Purchase, would double the size of the United States. The area needed to be explored because not much was known about it. Merriwether Lewis asked his friend William Clark to help him study the geography of the territory and report on the people, plants, and animals. The explorers made very good maps and kept superb diaries, enabling people today to picture what life in the territory was like at the time of Lewis and Clark.

Cause ______________________________

____

Effect ______________________________

____

Cause ______________________________

____

Effect ______________________________

____

Cause ______________________________

____

Effect ______________________________

____

Cause ______________________________

____

Effect ______________________________

____

At Home: Discuss an important journey or trip that one of your relatives or neighbors made. Be sure to include the results of the journey or trip.

Name ______________________________

As you read "A Historic Journey", fill in the Cause and Effect Chart.

Cause	→	Effect
	→	
	→	
	→	
	→	

How does the information you wrote in this Cause and Effect Chart help you make inferences and analyze "A Historic Journey"?

At Home: Have the student use the chart to retell the story.

Name ___________________________

As I read, I will pay attention to punctuation.

	Rachel Carson was born on May 27, 1907, in Springdale,
8	Pennsylvania. As a child, she loved exploring the fields and
18	woods around her home. Her mother shared Rachel's interest
27	in nature. She encouraged Rachel's curiosity. Rachel
34	observed the plants and animals and learned about them.
43	Even though she loved nature, Rachel was sure she would
53	be a writer when she grew up. She loved to read and listen to
67	stories. When she was 10, she wrote a story and sent it to a
80	children's magazine. Her story won an award. Rachel's
88	career as a writer had begun.
94	Even when she started college, Rachel still was sure that
104	she would be a writer. So, she planned to study English. But
116	one year she had to take a biology course. She liked it so
129	much that she decided to be a scientist. She took more
140	biology courses.
142	After graduating, Carson studied at Johns Hopkins
149	University. A few years later, she got a graduate degree in
160	zoology. She also spent the summers doing research at the
170	Marine Biological Laboratory in Woods Hole,
176	Massachusetts. There, Carson began observing the world of
184	the sea. She wanted to learn all she could about it. 195

Comprehension Check

1. What did Rachel Carson want to be when she grew up? **Main Idea and Details**
2. What changed her mind? **Summarize**

	Words Read	–	Number of Errors	=	Words Correct Score
First Read		–		=	
Second Read		–		=	

At Home: Help the student read the passage, paying attention to the goal at the top of the page.

Name ______________________

Find the following words in a dictionary or thesaurus. Answer the questions. Write the source in which you found the answer.

native	glimpse	entomology	buffalo
gully	trove	remote	vast

Question	Dictionary or Thesaurus?
1. Which word contains a Greek root meaning "insect"? ______________	
2. Which word can mean a "discovery," a "haul," or a "collection"? ______________	
3. Which word has three different acceptable ways to form the plural? ______________	
4. For which word are *lonely, isolated,* and *out-of-the-way* synonyms? ______________	
5. Which word means "trench" or "small valley"? ______________	
6. Which word is pronounced as just one syllable and means "to look at quickly"? ______________	
7. For which word are *giant* and *enormous* synonyms? ______________	
8. Which word contains a Latin root meaning "to be born"? ______________	

At Home: Ask a family member or helper to quiz you on the spellings and meanings of the above words.

Name ______________________

A. Read each word below. Then look in a dictionary or thesaurus to find an antonym for each word.

1. heroic ______________
2. locate ______________
3. combined ______________
4. diverse ______________
5. penniless ______________
6. display ______________
7. soaked ______________
8. stationary ______________
9. scorching ______________
10. sluggish ______________

B. Choose five pairs of words from above, and use each pair in a sentence with *but*.

11. ______________________________

12. ______________________________

13. ______________________________

14. ______________________________

15. ______________________________

At Home: Create a crossword puzzle using five pairs of antonyms.

Name ______________________________

Read the meanings of the prefixes below. Then write a meaning for each word and use it in a sentence.

dis-	(to do) the opposite of	*in-*	not
mis-	wrong	*pre-*	before

1. preview ______________________________

____

____

2. misinform ______________________________

____

____

3. disobey ______________________________

____

____

4. prehistoric ______________________________

____

____

5. disagreement ______________________________

____

____

6. inconsiderate ______________________________

____

____

At Home: Look for base words in newspapers and magazines and add the prefixes *dis-*, *in-*, *mis-*, and *pre-*.

Name ______________________________

Use your knowledge of the boldface vocabulary words to answer each question with a complete sentence. Use the boldface word in your sentence.

1. What is an **invasion**?

____

____

2. What is one reason why Navajo men **enlisted** to fight in World War II?

____

____

3. Where was the **location** of Grandfather's code-talking training classes?

____

____

4. How is a **reservation** different from other land?

____

____

5. Why would someone use a **shield**?

____

____

6. What does something that is **creased** look like?

____

____

7. Where might a **corridor** lead?

____

____

8. If a person's shoulders **sagged,** how might the person be feeling?

____

____

Name ______________________________

Read each passage from the story. Then answer the questions.

Grandfather sat down and began to speak gently in Navajo. The sounds wove up and down, in and out, as warm and familiar as the patterns of one of Grandmother's Navajo blankets. John leaned against his grandfather's knee.

1. How does this passage show the author's feelings about the characters and their relationships?

____

____

____

2. What are the author's feelings about the Navajo language?

____

____

____

"But why did you leave in the first place?" asked John.

His grandfather lifted him gently onto the horse. "The answer to that is in the code," he said. "The code name for America was 'Our Mother.' You fight for what you love. You fight for what is yours."

3. How does this passage show the author's feelings about America?

____

____

____

4. How does the tone of Grandfather's words suggest the author's opinions?

____

____

____

At Home: Read the opinions page in a newspaper and identify the author's perspective.

Name ______________________________

As you read *The Unbreakable Code,* fill in the Author's Perspective Chart.

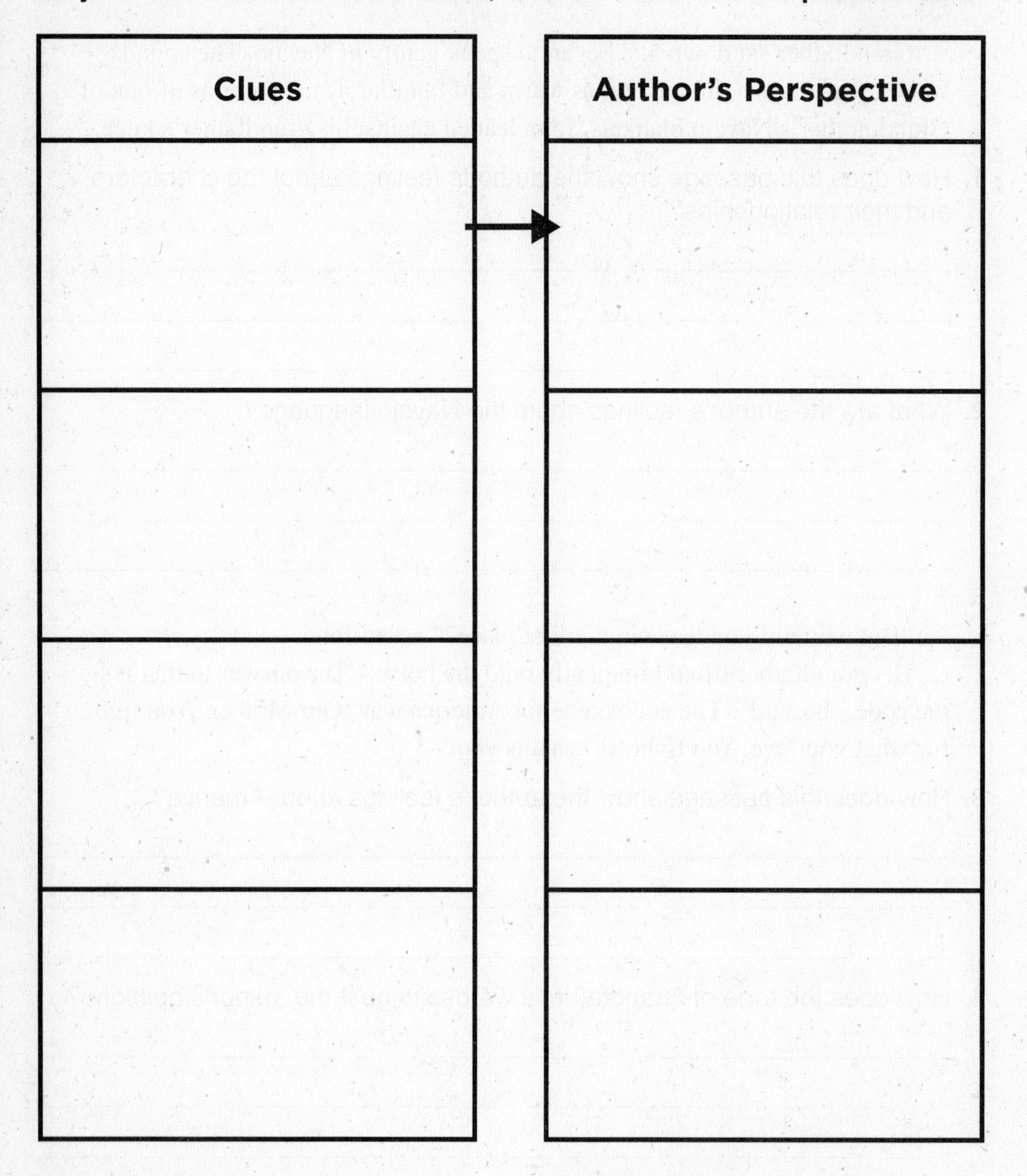

How does the information you wrote in the Author's Perspective Chart help you generate questions about *The Unbreakable Code*?

At Home: Have the student use the chart to retell the story.

Name ______________________________

As I read, I will pay attention to pauses and intonation.

	Throughout history, in every part of the world, civilizations have built
11	cities. They have made laws and created art. Some civilizations have
22	mysteriously disappeared. What happened to them? How can we uncover
32	their secrets?
34	Fortunately, the people who lived in many of these lost cultures left
46	clues behind. Tiny bits of writing have been discovered. These fragments
57	of writing are often the keys that can unlock the mystery of a lost culture.
72	All languages are codes. They are made up of words, letters, and/or
84	pictures that stand for something else. In the English language, the word
96	*hat* stands for something that you wear on your head. The number *5*
108	stands for a certain number of things. The letter *B* represents a sound
121	found in the word *ball* or *baby*.
128	Today, hundreds of languages are spoken around the world. To study
139	them, we can speak to the people who use these languages.
150	But some cultures are like locked boxes with missing keys. Their
161	languages cannot be read by anyone. The lives of the people who used
174	them remain unknown to us.
179	As long as there are codes to crack, experts will take language
191	fragments apart, piece by piece to try to find answers. 201

Comprehension Check

1. What clues do experts use to study lost cultures? **Main Idea and Details**

2. How are languages like codes? **Main Idea and Details**

	Words Read	–	Number of Errors	=	Words Correct Score
First Read		–		=	
Second Read		–		=	

At Home: Help the student read the passage, paying attention to the goal at the top of the page.

Name ______________________

Some poems have **consonance** and **symbolism**. Consonance is the repetition of the same consonant sound at the end of words. Symbolism is the use of concrete objects to represent or express abstract concepts, qualities, or ideas.

A. Read each cinquain below, then answer the questions.

Try to	1
Imagine this:	2
Dangerous night with stars	3
Cold stars different from the ones	4
Back home.	5

1. Which words in line 4 show consonance? ______________________
2. What might the different stars symbolize? ______________________

____

B. Write a paragraph explaining what consonance and symbolism add to poems.

____

____

____

____

____

____

____

____

At Home: List objects in your home or neighborhood that could be symbols of something else. Write a five-line poem about the object, using consonance.

Name ____________________

Context clues give hints about the meanings of unfamiliar words. Context clues can be in the same sentence as the unfamiliar word or in surrounding sentences.

Read the paragraph. Use context clues to help you figure out the meanings of the *boldface* words. Write definitions of the boldface words on the lines below.

The secret message was lying right beside me. But how would I ever **decipher** the secret code? I decided to call Mei and tell her my problem. Right away, I **recruited** her for the job of code breaker!

When I handed her the message, Mei went to work. She became **preoccupied** and fell into a deep state of concentration. After a while, I had to remind her that I was still there and that breaking the code did not have to be a **solitary** job! Still she was **persistent** and kept at it. After about half an hour she said, "I'm beginning to see a **recurrent** pattern here. Quick! I'll **dictate** my ideas about the things that repeat. Write down what I say."

I wrote down everything Mei said. Then she took my notes and **pondered** some more. At last, she said, "**Eureka**! I think I've got this **cipher** figured out!"

1. decipher ____________________
2. recruited ____________________
3. preoccupied ____________________
4. solitary ____________________
5. persistent ____________________
6. recurrent ____________________
7. dictate ____________________
8. pondered ____________________
9. Eureka ____________________
10. cipher ____________________

At Home: Look in a newspaper or magazine for unfamiliar words. Look up each word in a dictionary and use it in a sentence using context clues.

Name ________________________________

Practice

Phonics: Suffixes *-less* and *-ness*

Read the directions below to write a new word. Then use each word in a sentence.

1. Add a suffix to a base word to write a word that means "without fear."

____

____

2. Add a suffix to a base word to write a word that means "kind act."

____

____

3. Add a suffix to a base word to write a word that means "without effort."

____

____

4. Add a suffix to a base word to write a word that means "state of being weak."

____

____

5. Add a suffix to a base word to write a word that means "state of being foolish."

____

____

6. Add a suffix to a base word to write a word that means "without a bottom."

____

____

At Home: Look for five words in a newspaper or magazine that end with the suffixes *-less* and *-ness*. Use each word in a sentence and then circle the accented syllable.

Name ____

attraction	discussions	emerged	focused
inquire	ventured	sprawled	unreasonable

A. Use the words in the box to complete the passage below. Write your answers on the lines provided.

The bay in our town is famous as a great spot for whale-watching. In fact, during the summer, whale-watching trips are the town's main ________________ for tourists. The first whale-watching trip every year, however, is for town citizens only. Last year, I ________________ on the water and spotted the first whale as it ________________ from the sea.

This year there have been many ________________ about the upcoming whale-watching season. A group of scientists has arrived to study the whales, and their equipment is ________________ across the beach. Some people think it is ________________ of the scientists to take over the beach. In school, I ________________ to say that it was important that we learn as much as we can about the whales. My teacher suggested that I go to the beach and ________________ about what the scientists are trying to learn.

B. Write a new sentence for each of the following vocabulary words.

1. attraction: ____

____

____

2. discussions: ____

____

____

Name ____

A summary is a shortened and simplified version of a longer work. When you **summarize** a story, you give a brief summary or statement of what it is about.

Suppose that you are an assistant book critic for a magazine. It is your job to summarize each book that is reviewed. Think of a book that you especially liked. Write a summary of the plot and characters.

____

____

____

____

____

____

____

____

____

____

____

____

____

____

____

____

____

____

____

At Home: Summarize an article from a newspaper or magazine. Ask a family member or helper to compare your summary to the article.

Name ______________________________

As you read *The Gri Gri Tree,* fill in the Summary Chart.

Beginning

↓

Middle

↓

End

↓

Summary

How does the information you wrote in this Summary Chart help you generate questions about *The Gri Gri Tree*?

At Home: Have the student use the chart to retell the story.

Name ____________________

As I read, I will pay attention to tempo.

	"A whole weekend at Sunset Cove?" I asked, hardly believing
10	such good luck.
13	"Sure," my father answered. "You and Gregory deserve a weekend
23	at the beach, Melissa. After all, school starts next week, so this trip
36	will be our last adventure of the summer."
44	"Wow!" my brother Gregory cried. "When do we leave? Where
54	will we stay?"
57	"We'll leave as soon as we're packed," Dad said. "It's Friday, so
69	later this afternoon there could be lots of weekend traffic heading to
81	the beach. We'd better leave early, around noon, and then we'll be at
94	Sunset Cove by 3:00 or 3:30. We'll be staying at the Old Fisherman's
107	Inn, which is one of those beautiful little inns right on Shoreside
119	Avenue. I've heard the food is so good there that the place is a major
134	attraction for Sunset Cove visitors."
139	"What a great surprise!" I remember saying those words, even
149	though I had no idea just how surprising that weekend would be.
161	My brother Gregory and I are twins, and the following week we
173	would begin the sixth grade. Dad is a history professor at Bridgewater
185	College and had just started to write his new book, which is all about
199	Spanish explorers. 201

Comprehension Check

1. Why did Melissa's father want to leave for Sunset Cove as soon as possible? **Main Idea and Details**

2. What does Melissa's father do? **Main Idea and Details**

	Words Read	–	Number of Errors	=	Words Correct Score
First Read		–		=	
Second Read		–		=	

At Home: Help the student read the passage, paying attention to the goal at the top of the page.

Name ______________________________

Graphs are a way to compare data. Line graphs show how data changes over time.

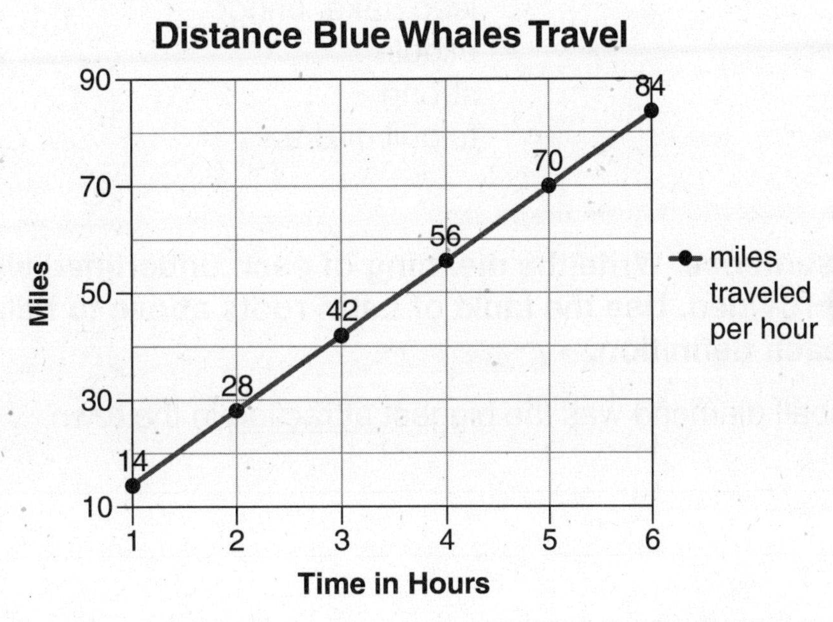

Blue whales are the largest animals on Earth. They usually swim 14 miles per hour but have been known to go as fast as 30 miles per hour.

Use the line graph to answer the questions.

1. How many miles total will the blue whale swim in 6 hours? __________
2. If a blue whale was swimming at 30 miles per hour, how many miles would it travel in 2 hours? __________
3. How many miles would a blue whale travel if it was swimming for 7 hours? __________
4. Why is this line graph useful? ______________________________

____

____

____

____

At Home: Add to this chart. Plot out how many miles a blue whale will travel in 9 hours.

Name ______________________________

Many word roots are Latin in origin. Here are some common **Latin roots** and their meanings.

Root	**Meaning**
duct	lead, take, bring
medius	middle
fortis	strong
tract	to pull or draw

Read each sentence. Write the meaning of each underlined word on the line provided. Use the table of Latin roots above to help you determine each definition.

1. The baseball diamond was the biggest attraction in the town.

____

____

2. The child's T-shirt was a medium size.

____

____

3. Let's fortify the shaky bridge with better supports.

____

____

4. The host will conduct everyone into the main dining room.

____

____

5. The army headed back to the safety of the fortification.

____

____

At Home: Use each underlined word above in a sentence.

Name ______________________________

Add *-ion* to each word below. Then write sentences using the words that you made.

1. elect ____________

2. correct ____________

3. prevent ____________

4. predict ____________

5. locate ____________

6. decorate ____________

7. concentrate ____________

8. discuss ____________

At Home: Look for ten words in a newspaper or magazine that end with *-ion*. Name the action words that they were formed from.

Name ______________________________

A. Read each description. Then choose a vocabulary word from the box, and write the word on the line at the left.

enlisted	uninhabited	frigid	dismantled	treacherous
abandon	unreasonable	traditional	inquire	discussions

1. ______________ taken apart
2. ______________ not lived in
3. ______________ dangerous
4. ______________ to leave without giving notice or to leave something behind
5. ______________ joined voluntarily
6. ______________ extremely cold
7. ______________ conversations about a subject
8. ______________ customary
9. ______________ to ask about
10. ______________ not able to be reasoned with

B. Write four sentences that include any four of the above vocabulary words.

11. ____

____

12. ____

____

13. ____

____

14. ____

____

Name ____________________

A. Read each word in column 1. Find its antonym, or the word most nearly opposite in meaning, in column 2. Then write the letter of that word on the line at the left.

	Column 1	Column 2
1. ____	combined	a. full
2. ____	vacant	b. straight
3. ____	complex	c. separate
4. ____	creased	d. hid
5. ____	emerged	e. simple
6. ____	sagged	f. raised

B. Complete each of the sentences below by using one of the vocabulary words from the box.

civilization location shortage strategy focused expedition

7. The brave explorers decided to go on an ________________ to the Arctic.

8. They lost some of their supplies, so there was a ________________ of food.

9. It is difficult to manage without the benefits of ________________, like a stable food source or government.

10. Thinking about how to solve a problem is easier when you are ________________ on it.

11. Maps usually show the correct ________________ of a place.

12. It's not a good idea to solve a problem without having a clear ________________.

Name ______________________________

Read each clue below to complete the crossword puzzle.

Across

3. went down

7. send away

8. agreed

Down

1. fine foods

2. plans

4. no hope

5. go with

6. headgear for a horse

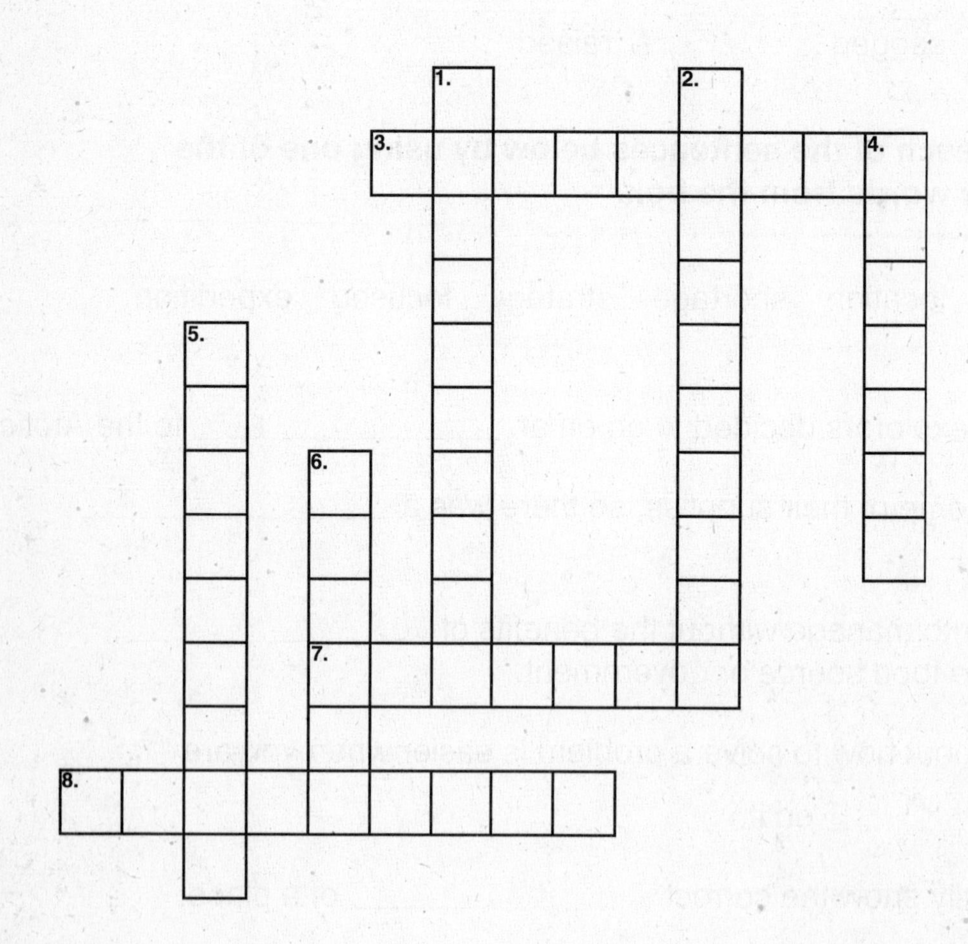

Name ____________________

A. Read the summary below of *The Golden Mare, the Firebird, and the Magic Ring.* Circle transitions such as *first*, *next*, *then*, and *finally*.

First, Alexi meets a golden mare. Next, the mare helps him to become the Tsar's huntsman. Later, Alexi brings the Firebird to the Tsar. Next, he brings Yelena the Fair to the Tsar. Finally, he brings Yelena's wedding ring to the Tsar. Yelena the Fair does not want to marry the Tsar, so she helps turn the Tsar into a baby. Then Alexi becomes the Tsar and marries Yelena the Fair. The first thing Alexi does as Tsar is order the release of the Firebird.

B. Use the transition words you circled above to help you figure out the correct sequence of events for those listed below. Then number the correct order of each event.

____ Alexi brings the Firebird to the Tsar.

____ Alexi becomes the Tsar and marries Yelena the Fair.

____ Alexi brings Yelena the Fair to the Tsar.

____ The Tsar is turned into a baby.

____ The golden mare helps Alexi become the Tsar's huntsman.

____ Alexi orders the release of the Firebird.

____ Alexi meets a golden mare.

____ Yelena's wedding ring is brought to the Tsar.

C. Answer the question.

Other than when reading a story, when is knowing a sequence helpful?

Why? ____________________

____

____

____

____

At Home: Identify a common sequence of events, and write the steps.

Name ____

Practice

Comprehension: Sequence

As you read *The Golden Mare, the Firebird, and the Magic Ring,* fill in the Sequence Chart.

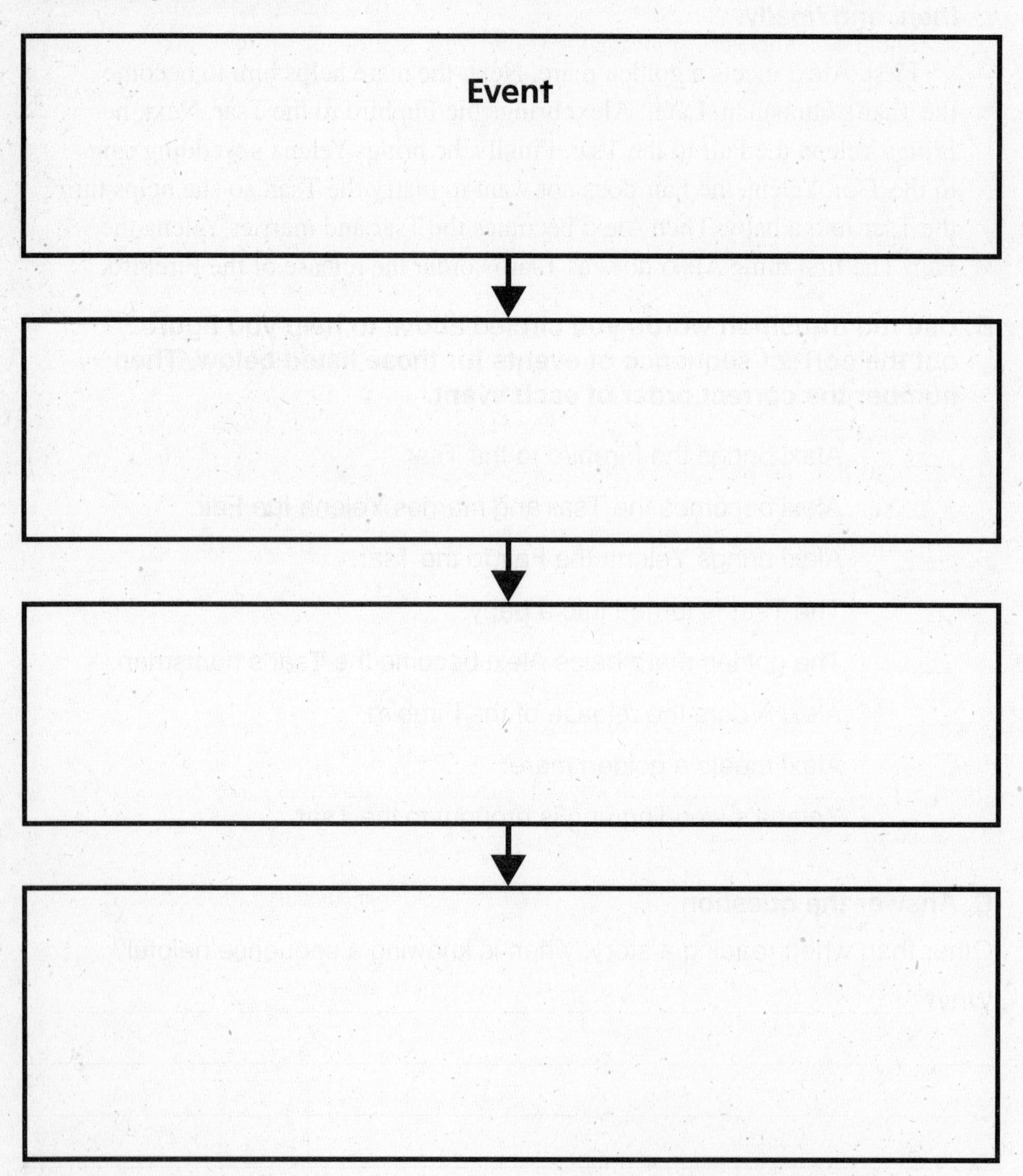

How does the information you wrote in this Sequence Chart help you summarize *The Golden Mare, the Firebird, and the Magic Ring*?

At Home: Have the student use the chart to retell the story.

Name ______________________________

As I read, I will pay attention to pauses and intonation.

Once upon a time, in a land far, far away lived a mother with her three
16 daughters and very young son. They lived on a beautiful old farm
28 surrounded by hills and mountains that were covered in wildflowers.
38 The mother loved flowers so much that when her daughters were born
50 she named each sweet child after a flower. Their names were: Rose,
62 Poppy, and Lily. The three girls grew into beautiful young women. They
74 were very smart, just like their mother. They loved to read and knew all
88 about the plants that grew around their home. They were often seen
100 walking the hills collecting flowers to study.
107 Every day, the daughters helped their mother. Rose cared for their
118 herd of sheep and goats. Poppy and Lily worked in the garden. They all
132 baked bread.
134 When the girls finished their chores, they went for walks collecting
145 plants. They drew pictures and took notes about each specimen they
156 found. They also talked, as sisters will on these walks. They talked about
169 their friends, school, flowers, and their dreams.
176 Rose, the eldest sister, loved the hardy plants that covered the cool
188 mountaintop. Her dream was to become an herbalist and discover new
199 medicinal uses for different herbs. 204

Comprehension Check

1. How did the three daughters get their names? **Main Idea and Details**

2. How did the daughters spend their days? **Summarize**

	Words Read	–	Number of Errors	=	Words Correct Score
First Read		–		=	
Second Read		–		=	

At Home: Help the student read the passage, paying attention to the goal at the top of the page.

Practice

Text Feature: Venn Diagram

Name ______________________________

Read the Venn diagram. Then, write a compare-and-contrast summary based on the information in the diagram.

Cinderella	Both	Rhodopis
evil stepmother and stepsisters, fairy godmother, prince, loses slipper at ball	household servants, lost slipper, kingdom is searched, end with marriage and happiness	pharaoh, animal friends, sings and dances, falcon finds slipper

____

____

____

____

____

____

____

____

____

____

____

____

At Home: Write your own fairy tale with elements shared by the Cinderella and Rhodopis stories. Refer to the Venn diagram for help.

Name ______________________________

Write the homophone. Then write a sentence for each word.

1. bridle ______________

2. grate ______________

3. mown ______________

4. prey ______________

5. lessen ______________

At Home: Find five or more words in newspapers or magazines that have homophones. List the words and their homophones.

Name ______________________________

Greek roots are found in many English words. A root is a small word part that usually cannot stand on its own.

Root	Meaning
astr/aster	star
auto	self
photo	light

Root	Meaning
phon	sound
mech	machine
graph	something written

Replace the underlined words in each sentence with one of the words from the box below, and rewrite the sentence.

mechanic	photometer	autograph
astronaut	phonics	biography

1. The author's <u>own signature</u> is on the first page.
____

2. Carla would like to meet the <u>person who travels to the stars</u>.
____

3. I will take the broken lawnmower to <u>the person who fixes machines</u>.
____

4. Knowing <u>rules about sounds and syllables</u> helps me read.
____

5. This <u>book about the life</u> of Abraham Lincoln is interesting.
____

6. The scientist used a <u>tool for measuring light</u> in her experiment.
____

At Home: Think of other words that include each of the roots above. Use each word in an original sentence.

Name ____________________

Answer each question in a complete sentence. Use the boldface word in your answer.

1. If something is **guaranteed** to happen, how likely is it?

2. If you were asked to **supervise** a hike, what might you do?

3. What has **frustrated** you about hiking or camping?

4. When would you need **coordination** at a campsite?

5. Why would you **ease** away from a skunk?

6. What **scenery** would you like to see on a camping trip?

7. What might you put in a **bundle** for a camping trip?

8. If marshmallows **fused** before you toasted them, what would you do?

Name ______________________________

Read each event below. Then answer each question.

1. The ranger gives Uncle Curtis a map of the campground. Uncle Curtis does not even glance at it. He throws it into the backseat. Do you think this behavior was a good idea?

____

____

____

2. When Uncle Curtis fails to find the campsite easily, he says, "They really ought to mark the campsite better." Do you think this is a reasonable comment considering the information from the first question?

____

____

____

3. The meat was packed in dry ice. When Uncle Curtis and the boys want to eat the meat, it is frozen solid. Do you think it was a good decision to pack the meat in dry ice?

____

____

____

4. Uncle Curtis says that nature lovers always share with one another. When Uncle Curtis needs firewood, other campers sell it to him for ten dollars. Why do you think the campers asked Uncle Curtis to pay?

____

____

____

At Home: Think about some decisions you've made lately about homework. Make judgments about whether your actions made sense and had the intended results.

Name ____

As you read *Skunk Scout,* fill in the Judgments Chart.

Action	→	Judgment
	→	
	→	
	→	
	→	

How does the information you wrote in this Judgments Chart help you monitor comprehension of *Skunk Scout*?

At Home: Have the student use the chart to retell the story.

Name ______________________________

As I read, I will pay attention to punctuation and inflection.

Yellowstone is in the heart of the American West. Its rivers
11 flow to both the East Coast and the West Coast. The Yellowstone
23 River starts south of the park. It flows to Yellowstone Lake and
35 then out of the park. Later the river joins up with the mighty
48 Missouri River, then the Mississippi, and finally the Gulf of
58 Mexico. Water that flows west out of Yellowstone Park
67 eventually ends up in the Pacific Ocean.
74 To find Yellowstone National Park on a map, look at the place
86 where northwestern Wyoming borders Montana and Idaho. In
94 fact, the park extends just a bit into both of those states.
106 For most people Old Faithful is the symbol of Yellowstone.
116 Old Faithful is a geyser from which heated water and air escape.
128 It gets its name from the fact that it erupts faithfully—
139 approximately every 60 to 120 minutes. It's been doing that for
148 well over 100 years—ever since people started taking notes.
157 When Old Faithful spouts, it's quite a sight! A plume of water
169 more than 100 feet high shoots into the air. 177

Comprehension Check

1. Yellowstone National Park is mostly located in which state? **Main Idea and Details**

2. Is the name Old Faithful appropriate? Explain. **Make Judgments**

	Words Read	–	Number of Errors	=	Words Correct Score
First Read		–		=	
Second Read		–		=	

At Home: Help the student read the passage, paying attention to the goal at the top of the page.

Name ______________________________

An **interview** is a way to gain information from someone. When you conduct an interview, you ask a person questions and he or she provides answers.

A. The author of your favorite book is coming to give a talk at your school. Write four questions that you would ask the author during an interview.

1. ______________________________

____

2. ______________________________

____

3. ______________________________

____

4. ______________________________

____

B. Write a summary based on how you think this author will respond to your questions.

____

____

____

____

____

____

____

____

____

At Home: Find an interview in a magazine. Write any questions that you would have asked that the interviewer did not.

Name ______________________________

Multiple-meaning words have several meanings. Context clues can help you figure out the meaning of the word.

Write two sentences for each word below, using different meanings of the word.

1. turn

____

____

2. patch

____

____

3. bear

____

____

4. rock

____

____

5. back

____

____

6. ground

____

____

At Home: Find five or more words in newspapers or magazines that are multiple-meaning words. Name two or more meanings for them.

Name ____________________

A. Study the root-word chart. Then write the root of each word.

Root Word	Meaning
aud	hear
spect	look at, see

Root Word	Meaning
port	carry
mit/miss	send

1. spectator ____________

2. auditorium ____________

3. intermission ____________

4. porter ____________

5. spectacular ____________

6. submit ____________

B. Use the clues below to find a new word. Then write a sentence containing the new word.

7. ex- (out) + port = ____________

____

____

8. miss + -ion (process of) = ____________

____

____

9. in- (in) + spect + -ion (process of) = ____________

____

____

10. in- (not) + aud + -ible (able) = ____________

____

____

At Home: List other words that have one or more of these roots. Then write sentences for each word.

Name ______________________________

A. Read each sentence beginning. Think about the meaning of the boldface vocabulary word. Then complete each sentence to show the meaning of the word.

1. If something is **elementary,** it is ______________________________
______________________________.

2. An example of a **physical** activity is ______________________________
______________________________.

3. A person who uses a **wheelchair** ______________________________
______________________________.

4. If your schedule is **rigid**, you ______________________________
______________________________.

5. You **interact** with your classmates when ______________________________
______________________________.

B. Write a paragraph about ways to improve lives. Use as many of the vocabulary words as possible.

____
____
____
____
____
____
____
____
____
____
____

Name ____________________

Read the following descriptions of techniques of persuasion. Design an ad in each space below, using one of the techniques.

Slogan: A catchy phrase or statement often used to sell a service or product.

Repetition: The name of a product is repeated many times.

Bandwagon: Sells products by stating that everyone is using it.

Testimonial: A well-known person supports a product or service.

Emotional appeal: A person is made to have strong feelings about a situation or product.

Technique of Persuasion: ____________________

Technique of Persuasion: ____________________

At Home: Write a paragraph that persuades someone to get involved in community events.

Name ____

As you read "A Dream Comes True", fill in the Fact and Opinion Chart.

Fact	Opinion

How does the information you wrote in this Fact and Opinion Chart help you monitor comprehension of "A Dream Comes True"?

At Home: Have the student use the chart to retell the story.

Name ______________________________

As I read, I will pay attention to pronunciation.

| | At the age of two, Anne contracted an eye disease called trachoma.
12 | By age five she was nearly blind. Anne's mother died when she was
25 | nine. After her father left the family, Anne and her young brother
37 | Jimmie were brought to the Tewksbury orphanage. It was a large and
49 | dreary building. Jimmie died there, and Anne who was only 10, was
60 | left alone in the world.
65 | But when Anne, known as Annie, turned 14, things began to get
76 | better for her. Annie pleaded to go to school. She wanted to learn.
89 | One man listened to her.
94 | Impressed by Annie's plea, the Boston philanthropist R.F. Sanborn
102 | arranged for her to go to the Perkins Institution, a school for the
115 | blind. At the school, Annie befriended Laura Bridgman. Laura had
125 | become famous because she was able to communicate even
134 | though she was deaf and blind. Many people visited the school to see
147 | the remarkable young woman. Annie learned to sign so that the two
159 | could **interact**. At first Annie hated the **rigid** rules of the school, but
172 | she loved to learn. By the time she finished school, Annie was
184 | number one in her class. 189

Comprehension Check

1. What challenges did Annie experience in her early life? **Summarize**

2. How did Annie's life change when she turned 14? **Summarize**

	Words Read	–	Number of Errors	=	Words Correct Score
First Read		–		=	
Second Read		–		=	

At Home: Help the student read the passage, paying attention to the goal at the top of the page.

Name ______________________________

We read **everyday communications** each day to find information about products, services, places, and people.

- Directions tell how to find a location.
- Consumer materials include instructions for a product.
- Brochures show and tell information about a place, product, or service in a way that is easy to read.
- Advertisements persuade you to buy, or give to something.
- Newsletters inform others about the activities of one particular group.

Write a short story in which the main character reads one example of each everyday communication. Underline the examples.

____

____

____

____

____

____

____

____

____

____

____

____

____

____

At Home: Design a brochure or write two kinds of consumer materials for a product or business.

Name ______________________________

Write the meaning of each bold word. List the context clues that you used to define the word.

1. People who run inside on **treadmills** never have to worry about the weather outside.

   Meaning: ______________________________

   ____

   Context clues: ______________________________

   ____

2. Vikram has a **rigid** exercise routine, and he never breaks it.

   Meaning: ______________________________

   Context clues: ______________________________

   ____

3. Studies show that children's activity levels start out high when they are young, but then **decline** and reach very low levels when they become older.

   Meaning: ______________________________

   Context clues: ______________________________

   ____

4. Satellite tools give **guidance** to the visually impaired, allowing blind people to go places on their own.

   Meaning: ______________________________

   Context clues: ______________________________

   ____

5. Our sailing teacher was a **gracious** person who tried to make everyone feel comfortable and welcome.

   Meaning: ______________________________

   Context clues: ______________________________

   ____

At Home: Find three unfamiliar words in a newspaper or magazine article and use each one in a sentence with context clues.

Name ______________________________

Practice

Phonics: Words from Mythology

Use the word origins in the left column to give the definitions of the words in the right column.

Words and Names from Myths	English Words and Meanings Today
Gaea was the Greek Earth goddess.	**geology**: ______________________ ______________________ **geography**: ______________________ ______________________
Kosmos was the Greek word for "order."	**cosmic:** ______________________ ______________________ **cosmetic**: ______________________ ______________________
The **Titans** were a family of giants in Greek mythology.	**titanic**: ______________________ ______________________
Vulcan was the Roman god of fire.	**volcano**: ______________________ ______________________ ______________________
Jove was a Roman god who controlled the seasons.	**jovial:** ______________________ ______________________
Atlas was a Greek Titan who had to hold up the world.	**atlas:** ______________________ ______________________

At Home: Find two more English words that are based on words or names from Greek or Roman mythology. For each word, make a dictionary entry.

Name ______________________________

A. Circle the vocabulary word that correctly completes the sentence.

1. At the moment, the hot air balloon is (anchored/launched) to the ground.
2. That woman and her (companion/hydrogen) will soon fly in the balloon.
3. In order to (anchor/inflate) the balloon, the air inside has been heated with propane.
4. Tiny (companions/particles) in the air are moving around quickly inside the balloon.
5. The air inside the balloon is hotter and lighter than the air outside, which is cool and (dense/scientific).
6. Let's wait here until the balloon is (anchored/launched) so that that we can see it rise.
7. Some balloons are used for pleasure, and others are used for (companion/scientific) purposes.
8. Balloons that do not carry people may be filled with the gas called (hydrogen/particles).

B. Write a definition for each vocabulary word.

9. anchored ______________________________
10. launched ______________________________
11. particles ______________________________
12. dense ______________________________
13. companion ______________________________
14. inflate ______________________________
15. scientific ______________________________
16. hydrogen ______________________________

Name ______________________________

Read the passage below.

The World's First Balloon Flight

Hot, smoky air rising from a fire had given Joseph Montgolfier an idea. Perhaps such air would make a balloon rise. Using small balloons, Joseph found that it did.

After many experiments, the Montgolfier brothers built a balloon that was about 30 feet across and 38 feet tall. It had a wooden frame at the base and was made of linen backed with paper. On June 5, 1783, near the city of Lyons, France, the Montgolfiers built a huge fire of damp straw and wool. Hot air poured into the base of the balloon. As a small crowd watched in amazement, the balloon envelope stirred, swelled, and finally rose upright.

Eight men were holding the balloon down. At a signal, they let go. It rose some 6,000 feet into the air and stayed aloft for ten minutes, landing gently in a nearby vineyard. This was the world's first balloon flight.

Make generalizations about the world's first balloon flight.

1. What generalization can you make about the differences between the first hot air balloons and modern hot air balloons? Explain your answer.

____

____

____

____

____

2. Write a generalization that describes Joseph Montgolfier as a person.

____

____

____

____

____

At Home: Think about an adventure or sport that is considered thrilling today, and make a generalization about why people love it.

Name ____

As you read *Up in the Air: The Story of Balloon Flight,* fill in the Generalizations Chart.

Information from Text	
Prior Knowledge	
Generalizations	

How does the information you wrote in the Generalizations Chart help you monitor comprehension of *Up in the Air*?

At Home: Have the student use the chart to retell the story.

Name ______________________________

As I read, I will pay attention to tempo and phrasing.

For thousands of years, people have been fascinated by the sky.
11 At night they looked up to see the moon and stars. In the daytime,
25 people observed the sun and cloud formations. In order to study the sky,
38 early scientists depended on a few simple tools—telescopes, kites,
48 balloons, and thermometers—to make their discoveries.
55 In 1749, Scottish scientist Alexander Wilson flew kites that carried
64 thermometers. The thermometers gave Wilson an idea of air temperatures
74 at different heights. A few years later Benjamin Franklin flew kites to
86 experiment with electricity.
89 Scientists have not been anchored to Earth since the late 1800s. They
100 have sent balloons and rockets into the air to gain knowledge. In 1892
112 the first weather balloons were flown in France. They measured
122 temperature, humidity, and air pressure.
127 Tools in the air also helped scientists learn more about Earth. Soon
139 after the first weather balloons, Swedish scientist Alfred Nobel
148 experimented with rockets. He designed one that flew up and
158 photographed the Earth.
161 Today scientific research takes place in Earth's atmosphere and
170 beyond. With advances in modern technology, scientists can fly into
180 raging storms. Weather balloons can soar high into the air. 190

Comprehension Check

1. Why is it useful that scientists use weather balloons and fly into storms? **Make Inferences**

2. How have kites been used as scientific tools? **Summarize**

	Words Read	–	Number of Errors	=	Words Correct Score
First Read		–		=	
Second Read		–		=	

At Home: Help the student read the passage, paying attention to the goal at the top of the page.

Name ____________________

A **simile** is a figure of speech in which one object is compared to another to suggest that they are alike. Similes contain the words ***like*** or ***as*** to connect the two objects.

A **metaphor** is a figure of speech in which one object is compared to another to suggest that they are alike.

Read the haiku, then answer the questions.

#1
The pilot writes lines
Like a poet in the air
Across the blue sky.

#2
The roaring sky chalk
Draws a thick white line of smoke
On the bright blue board.

1. Find the simile in the first haiku and tell what is being compared.

____

____

2. What does the first haiku describe? _______________

____

____

3. Find the metaphors in the second haiku and tell what are being compared.

____

____

____

____

4. What does the second haiku describe? _______________

____

____

At Home: Write your own haiku. Include a simile or metaphor in your poem.

Read each sentence. Use context clues and information from the chart to write a meaning for each underlined word.

Root	Meaning	Root	Meaning
bio	life	graph	write
hydro	water	mega	very large

1. This biography is about Joseph Montgolfier.

____

2. Pictographs are very ancient writing systems.

____

3. Early hot-air balloons were filled with hydrogen.

____

4. The scientists examined the megaspore with the microscope.

____

5. Learning biology can help us understand animals, but not hot-air balloons.

____

6. The balloonist plans to write her autobiography.

____

7. We saw the movie about hot-air balloons at the megaplex.

____

8. The new dam provided hydroelectric power.

____

At Home: Use each underlined word above in a sentence of your own.

Name ______________________________

A prefix is a word part that is added to the beginning of a word to change its meaning. These prefixes are **number prefixes**:

uni- (one) *bi-* (two) *tri-* (three) *cent-* (one hundred)

Replace the underlined word or words in each sentence with a word from the word box.

binoculars	unify	unique	trio	centimeter
centipede	biweekly	trilogy	century	unicycle

1. Is it difficult to ride a bike with one wheel? ______________

2. The employees are paid every two weeks. ______________

3. Use the instrument with two telescopes to see the bird. ______________

4. The group of three performed last night. ______________

5. Here are the separate parts we want to make one. ______________

6. The distance was just one one-hundredth of a meter. ______________

7. That sofa is certainly one of a kind. ______________

8. I recommend reading the three books in a series. ______________

9. The creature with one hundred legs moves slowly. ______________

10. What will happen during the next one hundred years? ______________

At Home: Make a list of five other words that contain a number prefix.

Name ______________________________

A. Write the word from the list that best completes each group.

specimens	erupted	murky	dormant
biology	scoured	research	observer

1. samples, examples, ________________
2. overflowed, exploded, ________________
3. cleared, cleaned, ________________
4. inactive, sleeping, ________________
5. witness, onlooker, ________________
6. studies, investigation, ________________
7. zoology, botany, ________________
8. dark, muddy, ________________

B. Write a paragraph about the type of work a scientist does. Use as many of the vocabulary words as you can.

____

____

____

____

____

____

____

____

____

____

Name ______________________________

Use the sequence of events to retell major events in the life of Dennis Kunkel in time order. Add transitions such as *first, next, then, after,* and *later,* as well as any other details that you think are needed.

received his first microscope when he was 10

looked through the microscope to study prepared (dead) specimens

began to go on trips to collect live specimens

went to college, where he was able to use good microscopes and speak with others about science

went to graduate school and began to use an electron microscope for his own research

earned a Ph.D. in botany (the study of plants)

was part of a team that explored Mount St. Helens after it erupted

____
____
____
____
____
____
____
____
____
____
____
____
____

At Home: Retell a sequence of events in the life of an older relative or another adult you know well.

Name ______________________________

Practice

Comprehension: Sequence

As you read *Hidden Worlds* fill in the Sequence Chart.

Event

↓

↓

Event

↓

↓

How does the information you wrote in the Sequence Chart help you summarize *Hidden Worlds*?

At Home: Have the student use the chart to retell the story.

Name ______________________________

As I read, I will pay attention to pauses and intonation.

Much of the energy people use comes from oil and coal.
11 Oil and coal are fossil fuels. They were made inside the
22 earth from dead plants and animals.
28 Fossil fuels powered many of the advances of the last 200
38 years. They sent trains rumbling down tracks and planes
47 zooming into the sky. They supplied power to run factories.
57 But fossil fuels create a lot of pollution. And sooner or later,
69 they will run out.
73 Scientists are searching for alternatives to replace fossil fuels.
82 Some kinds of alternative energy have been used for thousands
90 of years. Others are only just beginning to be discovered.
102 Fossil fuels helped the modern world grow. But as an
112 energy source, fossil fuels are far from perfect. For one
122 thing, the supply of oil and coal is limited. The oil that is
135 being used now was made many millions of years ago. When
146 this oil is gone, it cannot be replaced. Some observers
156 believe that the world's supply of oil will be gone in 50 years.
168 No big new oil fields have been found since the 1970s.
178 And when new oil fields are found, they contain lower
188 quality oil. The oil is also harder to get at. 198

Comprehension Check

1. How are fossil fuels made? **Main Idea and Details**

2. Why are scientists searching for alternatives to replace fossil fuels? **Main Idea and Details**

	Words Read	–	Number of Errors	=	Words Correct Score
First Read		–		=	
Second Read		–		=	

At Home: Help the student read the passage, paying attention to the goal at the top of the page.

Name ________________________________

Read the outline below of the basic parts of a myth told by the Cowlitz people. Then write a myth using symbolism and figurative language.

Characters: Mount Rainier, the largest and most dangerous volcano in the Cascades, Mount St. Helens, and Mount Adams

Conflict: Mount Rainier had two wives. One of the wives, Mount St. Helens, was very jealous.

Event: Mount Rainier had an argument with his two wives.

Event: Mount St. Helens, whom the Cowlitz called "Smoking Mountain," became very jealous.

Event: Mount St. Helens knocked Mount Rainier's head off.

Resolution: The top of Mount Rainier does not come to a point. Even though Mount Rainier has very steep sides, it is somewhat flat across the top.

____

____

____

____

____

____

____

____

____

____

____

____

At Home: Look through a favorite book for more symbolism and figurative language.

Name ______________________________

Many roots and other word parts have Latin or Greek origins. For example, *-logy* is a Greek word part and can mean "science of." *Script* or *scrib* is a Latin root and means "to write."

Follow the directions below to create word families. Some words may change spelling. Write each new word and its meaning.

The *-logy* Word Family

1. geo (earth) + *-logy* = ______________________________

2. bio (life) + *-logy* = ______________________________

3. hydr (water) + *-logy* = ______________________________

4. psych (mind) + *-logy* = ______________________________

5. techn (skill) + *-logy* = ______________________________

The *script/scrib* Word Family

6. pre + *script* + -ion = ______________________________

____

7. de + *scrib* = ______________________________

____

8. *scrib* + le = ______________________________

____

9. post + *script* = ______________________________

____

10. in + *script* + -ion = ______________________________

____

At Home: Find one or more other members in each of the word families.

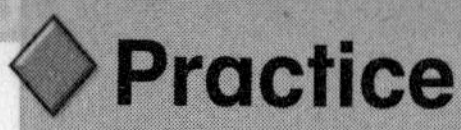

Name ______________________________

Phonics: Words with *-able*, *-ible*

Make new words by adding *-able* or *-ible* to each base word or root below. Then write a sentence using each new word.

1. suit + -able = ____________ ______________________

____

2. afford + -able = ____________ ______________________

____

3. convert + -ible = ____________ ______________________

____

4. like + -able = ____________ ______________________

____

5. favor + -able = ____________ ______________________

____

6. poss + -ible = ____________ ______________________

____

7. vis + -ible = ____________ ______________________

____

8. use + -able = ____________ ______________________

____

9. comfort + -able = ____________ ______________________

____

10. collapse + -ible = ____________ ______________________

____

At Home: With a family member or helper, look in newspapers for other words that end in *-able* or *-ible.*

Name ______________________________

A. Answer each question. Use the vocabulary word in your answer.

1. Have you ever eaten any **delicacies**? Give an example of one.

____

2. Under what conditions do you think an employer should **dismiss** an employee?

____

3. How would a **rigid** judge decide a case?

____

4. At what age do children usually begin **elementary** school in your state?

____

5. How would you make a path through a **dense** forest?

____

B. Supply the correct vocabulary word.

accompany	intentions	supervise	physical	companion

6. My little brother was too young to eat by himself, so I had to ______________ him.

7. He had good ______________ to help but only made the mess worse.

8. A pet can be a good ______________ for someone who lives alone.

9. In order to prepare for the race, the man ran, lifted weights, and did other ______________ activities to stay in shape.

10. Debbie will ______________ Chris to the prom as his date.

Name ______________________________

A. Use each of the vocabulary words in the box to make a sentence of your own.

observer	research	erupted	scenery	interact

1. ____
____

2. ____
____

3. ____
____

4. ____
____

5. ____
____

B. Read each word in column 1. Find its antonym, or the word that is most nearly opposite in meaning, in column 2. Then write the letter of that word on the line.

Column 1	Column 2
6. consented ____	**a.** ascended
7. frustrated ____	**b.** whole
8. descended ____	**c.** landed
9. particles ____	**d.** refused
10. launched ____	**e.** aided